John Baker Hopkins

The Fall of the Confederacy

Vol. 1

John Baker Hopkins

The Fall of the Confederacy
Vol. 1

ISBN/EAN: 9783337330965

Printed in Europe, USA, Canada, Australia, Japan

Cover: Foto ©ninafisch / pixelio.de

More available books at **www.hansebooks.com**

CONTENTS.

PAGE

PREFACE v

CHAPTER I.

THE CALL FOR INQUIRY 11

CHAPTER II.

THE REVOLUTION WAS UNTIMELY 25

CHAPTER III.

THE WAR WAS PRECIPITATE 37

CHAPTER IV.

THE CONFEDERATE POLICY 51

CHAPTER V.

NEGRO EMANCIPATION . . . 63

CHAPTER VI.

THE VERDICT 79

CHAPTER VII.

THE FUTURE OF THE UNION 86

PREFACE.

CLEAR-SIGHTED and stout-hearted men sometimes feared that the late conflict in America was but the beginning of woes unto the English-speaking race. There was apprehension of so dire a calamity as war between England and America. War between two nations that are indissolubly one by nature, circumstances, and interest. War between two nations so associated, that what injures the one harms the other. There is every possible motive for peace between them; nor can there be suggested a colourable motive for hostility. The peoples of England and America are of one race and of one descent. Nay, the kinship is yet nearer, they are of one family; they speak one language; they have a common literature; they profess the same Holy Faith; their liberties were bought with the blood and heroism of a common ancestry. It is not an exaggeration to assert that these twain nations of one flesh have all things in common. The laws of America and the laws of England so accord in principles, that he who has mastered one code, can readily practise in the Courts of either country. America is a Republic, and England is a Monarchy, yet one Constitution is a counterpart of the other. The English government is a Democratic Constitutionalism, whilst the American government is a Constitutional Democracy. In England the Chief Magistrate is an hereditary sovereign; and in America, an elected President; but neither the Monarch of England nor the President of America has any other than defined executive authority. In both countries public opinion is predominant—here represented by the Press and by Parliament; and in America by the Press and by Congress. The two nations have common aspirations and common faults. Both are ambitious; both love a wide domain; both carry their commerce to the ends of the earth, and crowd the seas with their fleets; both are exceedingly sensitive, and are rashly extreme to mark and to resent real or supposed insults. These, and many other bonds unite England and America, and strong as any, or all other bonds together, is the complete identity of interest. Their only reasonable rivalry is in the arts of peace, for the one wants nothing of the other that can be gained by war. Divided the English-speaking race may lag behind other races, but united no foe can hurt it, or will dare assail it. When shall we be delivered from the plague of an armed peace, the progenitor as well as the harbinger of wars to come? An armed peace is war, with all the ills of war, save the horrors of the battle-field. It depresses the springs of industry and commerce. It is the blight of nations, and the social cancer. To it must be ascribed the poverty, the destitution, and the vice that disgraces our vaunted civilisation. It is an armed peace that fills the workhouse and the jail, and that crowds the streets with fallen women. An armed peace does the work of anti-Christ. Is there a hope of deliverance? Yes; in the complete union of the English-speaking race. Let it be known that England and America are one in defence of their several rights, and England may set an example of disarmament, even on the sea; and the example must be followed. If England reduces her armaments the continental Powers must do likewise, for the peoples would not, could not, endure the continuance of a system needless for defence, needless even for aggression, and which would make it impossible for them to compete with England in industry and commerce.

There has been much distrust and bickering between England and America, and mainly because the one nation has misunderstood the other. The distrust is only superficial. Englishmen — and indeed Englishwomen too—have a mania for personal banter or chaff. They have laughed and quizzed Americans and sometimes irritated our cousins, who would not regard it if they were aware that in Parliament, and even in the Courts of Justice, Englishmen cannot restrain their propensity for chaffing. On the other hand, Englishmen are offended at what they call American brag. Now the brag is not more irritating than the chaff, and is not intended to be offensive. There is not more harm in American "tall talk" than there is in English chaff. After all, England loves America, and America loves England. Let an Englishman fall in with a Frenchman or a German, and if the conversation turn upon America he will indulge in the loudest boast of what his kindred have done in the New World. Or let an English traveller, or an English author, or an English worthy of any sort visit America, and he will be overwhelmed with hearty and boundless hospitality and attention. Or speak to any American of any party about Queen Victoria, and touching is the manifestation of respect —of affectionate respect—which the mention of her name will evoke.

The late war in America was a trying crisis for the friendship of England and America; and it may be that still there exists some ill-will in reference to the conduct of England. The Abolitionists were angry that any party in England sympathised with the slave-holding South. Now, assuredly, if it had been known that the North was fighting for Emancipation, and the South for Slavery, there would not have been a pro-Southern party in England. Then there was discontent because England recognised the Confederates as belligerents. Now, the recognition of belligerentcy was not on account of the claims put forth by the South that they had a right to separate from the North. It was on the part of the English Government a mere recognition of a *de facto* state of warfare. The recognition of belligerentcy would not have been deemed so unfriendly by the North had this been thoroughly understood. But it was represented as an admission of the validity of the impracticable and pernicious Southern doctrine of State Rights, a doctrine which is discussed in the last chapter of this Essay. Further, it is alleged that England was guilty of a breach of neutrality in respect to Confederate cruisers. May it be long before America learns by experience how difficult it is to prevent infringements of the laws of neutrality. It is not to be denied that much was said and written that was unkind to the United States. England has this excuse, that it was a period of intense excitement, that Englishmen devoted all their thoughts to the war in America, and that, as in America, so in England, there was divided opinion and fierce partizanship. But England offended the South as well as the North, for the South was incensed that there was not national recognition, which meant intervention. We are sure that a candid consideration of the causes that led to the fall of the Confederacy will, in the minds of the Southern people, fully exonerate England. Further, it will set us right with the whole people of America, whilst it will satisfactorily explain to Englishmen the irritation of America at our conduct. The writer has been expecting, from month to month, that the subject would be treated by an able pen;

and it is with great diffidence that he submits this Essay to the consideration of his friends in England and America. A prefatory word may be expedient respecting the chapter on the future of the Union. The writer does not presume to offer an opinion upon the Government of America to Americans. His object is to combat what he deems the erroneous views that are entertained by some Englishmen respecting the position and prospects of the United States.

JOHN BAKER HOPKINS.

FALL OF THE CONFEDERACY.

CHAPTER I.

THE CALL FOR INQUIRY.

At the outset of this inquiry it is imperative to define its objects and limits with the utmost precision. We are not about to intrude on the domain of history. We do not profess to tell the story of the American war. We propose to hold an inquest on the late Confederacy, and, if possible, to discover the immediate causes of death. We shall offer no opinion upon the merits of the quarrel that convulsed a continent, and for four years absorbed the attention of the civilized world. We shall signally fail in our object if any one can tell from these pages whether we sympathized with the North or with the South. Yet this investigation will not be found dull, or if so, it will be owing to our treatment of an event grand enough to distinguish the ninteenth century, and which has already exercised an enormous influence in directing and revolutionising the affairs of America and of Europe. We hope to be able to demonstrate the abstract right and pressing expediency of discussing the immediate causes of the Fall of the Confederacy. To ascertain the truth in this case, and to declare it, is a solemn duty we owe to the memory of the dead, to the living, and to posterity.

In its long secretion, in its discovery, and in its history, America is a land of marvels. It is now in hourly communication with Europe; yet, until the fourteenth century of the Christian era, the existence of what is fitly called the New World was unknown and unsuspected.

America first appeared as a dreamland. The adventurers who had approached its shores, and seen the isles that surround it like satellites, invented strange stories about this their fabled India. It was a land of silver mountains, and of rivers whose crystal waters rippled over sands of gold. The ivory palaces of its kings were studded with countless gems, each one outvaluing a prince's ransom, and flashing forth blinding lightnings as they reflected the rays of a torrid sun. The trees, of prodigious size and exuberant foliage, were inhabited by birds of gorgeous plumage, whose song was as the song of seraphs. The climate was so finely tempered that there was neither pain nor sickness. There grew the plant from which might be distilled the long-sought *elixir vitæ*—the potion that would impart perpetual youth and baffle grim death. The women were of exceeding beauty. The men were warriors. There were dwarfs of unheard of smallness. There were giants tall as the trees of Europe. There were one-eyed tribes—the single eye flaming in the midst of the forehead. There were two-headed tribes. There were sorcerers, whose fell deeds were told with bated breath. There were spell-bound princesses, whose deliverers would wed a royal maiden and receive an empire for dowry. The most heated imagination could not conceive a story about the fabled Indian that would have seemed incredible to the Columbian age.

Yet let us beware how we sneer at the credulity of those times. Are not the realities of the New World more marvellous than the wild fairy-like fictions of the adventurers? America is, indeed, a land in which nature has secreted exhaustless treasures. From the bowels of the earth well up a constant streams of oil, fit for light and fuel, and that promises, by the aid of chemists, to form a substitute for coal that will enable steamers to perform the longest voyages with ample stock of food for the furnace. America has silver mines, the most prolific in the world. Her yield of gold exceeds the dreams of the Columbian adventurers. But the yield of gold contributes but a little to the greatness and riches of the New World. It is at best a helpmeet, but not a basis of modern commerce. And is not the story of modern commerce more wonderful than the story of silver mountains, of rivers flowing over beds of gold, of palaces of ivory, and of priceless gems dazzling as orient suns? The dreary waste of waters over which Columbus sailed has become a frequented highway. Reposing in the depths of the Atlantic are cables by which Europe and America are able to speak to one another. It is modern commerce that has given to science the power to achieve this and a hundred triumphs by which heretofore distant countries have been united and become near neighbours. Thanks to modern commerce the working man of this generation has physical comforts that two centuries ago wealth could not buy. But grander still are its intellectual and moral trophies. To it we owe modern civilization. It has carried Christianity to the uttermost parts of the earth. The political freedom of which we boast, the spread of knowledge in which we glory, are the offspring of modern commerce. Surely thus to raise and exalt mankind are incomparably nobler achievements than could have resulted from the discovery of a land of gold, silver, and precious stones.

And what are the chief bases of modern commerce? The trade in cotton, tea, tobacco, and sugar. Now it is from America that we get the main supplies of cotton, sugar, and tobacco, and it is the cotton of America that has opened the tea-market of China. Take away the cotton, sugar, and tobacco of America and the whole fabric of modern commerce would as surely totter as without them it surely could not have been built up. It is then to the discovery of the New World that we are indebted for modern commerce, and the countless and priceless benefits that proceed from it. But the age that believed the fairy-like tales of the adventurers would not have believed a prophetic revelation of the story of modern commerce. Would the incredulity have been unreasonable? Shall we then sneer at the credulity which believed in stories that were false, but which were not so marvellous as the truth?

But not less certain or less reasonable would have been the incredulity, if a prophet had foretold the political and social career of the vast Republic which dominates in the New World. A few old men are yet in the flesh who were in the cradle when the

United States, ceasing to be colonies, had just been born into the family of nations. Suppose, at the outset of the war of independence, some one had told the King of England that in less than threescore years and ten—the allotted span of human life, but a day in the life of a nation—the handful of colonists would have become one of the greatest of the Great Powers. Not only the Third George, but also the most sagacious of his subjects, would have treated the prediction with contempt. The King wept, as well he might, to lose thirteen colonies. How would his grief have been intensified if he could have had a vision of the future of those colonies! There would have been no consolation for him. For if some one could have told him that his grand-daughter would be Queen of the Canadas—Queen of the newest world that is washed by the Pacific—Empress of India, and the mistress of two hundred millions of people, the prediction would have been regarded as a cruel and bitter mockery in the hour of disaster.

But we need not cite events that are even one generation old to prove that the history of America has been so strange as to refute predictions founded on experience, and that the apparently probable has not come to pass, and the apparently impossible has been realised. Imagine some writer of eminence stating, in January 1860, that he believed the then impending party conflict would be followed by a disruption of the Union, by a four years' civil war—a war that would cost more treasure than the long Continental war cost England, and would involve an unsurpassed sacrifice of human life. Why, the writer, despite his eminence, would have been laughed at, and no one would have deemed it worth while to reply to his speculations.

Yet all this happened, and further, almost every incident of the contest belied anticipation.

In four years we beheld the birth, the eventful life and the sudden death of the Confederacy. In the summer of 1860 it was not even in embryo. It was born in 1861. In the summer of 1862 it was a power with a quarter of a million of men under arms. In the summer of 1865 the Confederacy had become historical. The world looked on with eager unfaltering interest. The stage was a continent, the actors were peoples and races. Upon the result of the conflict depended the fate of the negro race, the future of the United States, of Mexico, and indeed all the continent was to be directly or indirectly, immediately or hereafter, affected by the issue of a contest than which none more fierce, gigantic, and momentous was ever waged.

By means of telegraphy, steam, and a press that may be described as ubiquitous, men afar off were able to watch from day to day the short life of the Confederacy. Yet no one was quite prepared for the catastrophe when it came. The Confederacy was sick with a mortal sickness. She was in the death-agony. So far there was no misconception. But few thought that the agony was so shortly to terminate in annihilation.

For nearly four years the Confederacy was a considerable power. She equipped armies. She carried on a mighty warfare. Her flag was borne on the high seas. Her securities were quoted on the Exchanges of Europe. In the early spring of 1865 she was still in being. The second session of her second Congress was being held in her capital. The illustrious Lee, though hard-pressed, was unconquered, True, there were signs of weakness. The South, that is, the generals, the statesmen, and the people, were not deceived by the defiant tone of the Government, for they knew that the Confederacy was in the throes of dissolution. The soldiers were conscious that their lives were being offered up in vain. But surely no one imagined that the death-agony would be so soon over, and that the instant of decease was so near at hand. No one imagined that in a few days the Confederacy would not only have fallen, but would be dead, buried, and altogether a thing of history. But it was so. Long ere the same early spring had ripened into summer, the Federal flag waved over Charleston, the Federal forces were in Richmond, Lee surrendered, the Confederate Administration was fugitive, and the Confederacy was clean gone.

What was the immediate cause of death? Was it heart disease? Was it brain disease? Was it disease of the blood? Was it shear inanition? It concerns both North and South, it concerns the re-united Republic, it concerns all of us to ascertain this. The Confederacy is so thoroughly historical that we can enter upon the investigation without any feeling of partizanship. Yet the Confederacy was so lately living that we have an unprecedented opportunity for making the *post-mortem* of a deceased power.

We have in this inquiry nought to do with the morality or immorality of the Confederacy. If the cause was good that is a reason for regretting, but does not account for the failure. If the cause was evil that is a reason for rejoicing in the success of the North, but does not necessarily explain the overthrow of the Confederacy.

Probably the general response will be that the superior numbers and resources of the North rendered her triumph inevitable. This may or may not be true in part, but to accept it in its entirety would be most unfair to both belligerents, and would be a dangerous and demoralising conclusion. Is numerical superiority *per se* always omnipotent? Shall we declare that a minority cannot, under any circumstances, assert its real or imagined rights with a hope or chance of triumph? It is, indeed, a sound doctrine that other forces being equal, superior numbers will prevail. Were the other forces so equal that the failure of the Confederacy was a foregone conclusion? The respective numbers and resources were known at the beginning of the conflict, and if the superior numbers of the North made the failure of the Confederacy inevitable, the Confederate Administration was guilty of a huge and detestable crime in commencing and carrying on a contest that could only desolate the country and cause a fearful waste of life. But to rebut so foul a charge the Confederate Administration might appeal to many chapters of history which record the triumphs of minorities. In the providential government of the world, forces are frequently brought into play that overcome superior numbers, and therefore the victory is not always gained by the side which is numerically the stronger. Christianity, civilization, political development, and liberty are the victories of sometime minorities. As a rule, might is allied to right, and when right fails it is, we may be sure, because right has neglected to enlist or has misused her forces. Since the fall of the Confederacy there has been a growing tendency to worship the power of mere numbers, which may have some disastrous consequences. It will, therefore, be of vast service if it can be shown that however probable the ultimate triumph of the North, the immediate cause of the fall of the Confederacy was not the numerical superiority of her antagonist.

Besides, it is a gross libel to assume that the North gained the victory solely on account of her superior numbers. Who, duly considering the circumstances, will be so unjust to the genius, the perseverance, and the high spirit of the North? Not the Confederate Administration, for then they would be self-branded with infamy for beginning and continuing a hopeless conflict. The North did not gain an easy victory. Her defeat was always possible, and would have been certain but for her determination, her valour, and her immense sacrifices of life and property. For nearly four years there was a harassing strain upon the resources of the country. Any faltering would have been fatal. A people prone to violent political partizanship, forgot all party differences, or at least made them secondary to the prosecution of the war. A trading community became so lavish of its gold that it ceased to count the cost of the costliest conflict of the century. A nation accustomed to the most unrestrained liberty gave virtually despotic power to its chief magistrate. A nation peculiarly sensitive with regard to its foreign relations kept the peace with Europe in spite of some actual or apparent provocations. Had the North failed in one of these things, had she been niggardly, or divided, or hesitating, or incapable of controlling her feelings of anger and resentment, then the Confederacy would not have died in 1865. Without superior numbers the North might have been unsuccessful; and even with her superior numbers she would not have succeeded as she did had it not been for the exercise of those virtues and talents which in all ages and countries are the source and support of national greatness, and to which are due the might, the majesty, and the glory of the English-speaking race.

It may be said that the Confederate Administration ought to have known in advance that the people of the North would act as they did act, and that, therefore, the superior numbers of the North would be triumphant. Perhaps so. The Confederate Administration was perhaps unwarranted in supposing that the North would not fight for the Union, that the West would not join with the East, that the Northern people would not incur a heavy war debt, and that foreign powers would intervene. We must, however, allow that the Confederate Administration had some expectation of contingencies that would redress the disparity of numbers and resources. They were sensible that superior numbers would, if not met with counter-balancing forces, succeed. We have to inquire how the expectation of success was so frustrated, that in less than four years the Confederacy died. One conclusion, we are confident, will be arrived at by all impartial inquirers. It is, that the immediate cause of the fall of the Confederacy was not the superior numbers of the North.

And here let us hasten to do justice to the Southern people. Who will be so grievously unfair as to blame them for the fall of the Confederacy? Were they half-hearted? Did they fail the Confederate Administration? Did they shrink from the needful sacrifice of life and property? Those who are now their fellow-citizens, and who then stood against them as enemies, will not utter so foul a calumny. No people ever endured greater toils and privations than the people of the South. Pinched by famine, oppressed by defeat, they fought on bravely. Nay, when they saw that the cause was lost, they still obeyed the voice of the Confederate Administration, and went forth without murmuring, to fight like heroes, and to die like martyrs. They maintained a bold defiant attitude when death, want, and disease had so thinned their ranks that between the Confederacy and destruction was but one faint line of veterans. No; it was not the people of the South that failed the Confederacy. It was the policy of the Confederate Administration that ensured and hastened its doom. As we shall presently notice, the Confederacy was born before the revolution, and it survived the revolution. It was a generous sentiment of loyalty that prevented the South from ending the struggle in 1864. No sooner did Lee sheath his sword, than the whole people bowed to the decision, and gave up all resistance. This would not have happened if the Confederacy had continued to represent a revolution. But the Confederate Administration, which in 1861 invoked a revolution to support the Confederacy, had by its policy killed the revolution at least a year before the Confederacy fell.

Likely enough there will be a sneer at this bill of indictment against the Confederate Administration, on the ground that it is easy to be wise after the event. Doubtless the story of the Confederacy should teach us a lesson of humility. The predictions of the keenest intellects have been signally refuted. Even those who from the beginning prophesied the success of the North were wrong in many of their surmises. When the first mutterings of the storm were heard it was said that the South might bluster, but would not really secede, yet a few weeks after the election of Mr. Lincoln the Confederacy was formed. After secession the idea of war was ridiculed, Europe smiled at the bloodless fall of Sumter, yet such a war ensued that Europe was shocked at its horrible proportions. It was assumed that the Confederacy would do nothing on the sea, yet she crippled the mercantile marine of the North, and gained a victory in Hampton Roads that demonstrated the superiority of iron over wood, and changed the system of naval warfare throughout the world. It was said that the negroes would rise against their masters, but they set an example of social fidelity and patient endurance to all peoples and races. It was said that the Union party in the South would declare itself, but until the war was over there was no manifestation of unionism. The seaports and the border cities of the South were to fall in the first campaign, and the war was to be carried on in the interior, but the outposts were held until the last, and when they fell, the Confederacy ceased to exist. We were assured that if the armies of the Confederacy were defeated the fires of revolution would smoulder for years, and that it would require as great an army to hold the South as it did to conquer the Confederacy, but when Lee surrendered all resistance ceased, and the North was able forthwith to disband her armies. When the armies were disbanded, there were to be hosts of men unfitted for civil employment, roving over and pillaging the country, but the disbanded soldiers of all ranks returned immediately to the pursuits of peace. The North was to stagger under a load of debt, and to grow faint-hearted by the loss of life, but she piled up a stupendous debt with cheerfulness, and raised army after army with unrivalled alacrity. It was suggested that the Southerners were too enervated to make good soldiers, but they fought with a splendid and unrivalled heroism. It was hinted that the Northerners were traders, who would shrink from the toils of war, but they showed themselves compeers of the soldiers of the South in bravery and endurance. It was said that there was a complete dearth of military talent in the North, but Grant and Sherman proved themselves worthy antagonists of such captains as Stonewall Jackson and Robert Lee. The Southern climate was to decimate the Northern armies, but the yellow fever did not appear, and probably never did invaders suffer so little from pestilence. It was supposed that England would be so crippled by the loss of her cotton trade that she would be goaded into intervention, but though there was distress in Lancashire, the total trade of the country increased, and the war that was to have impoverished, added to the wealth of England.

We have by no means exhausted the list of mistakes. It is not to be denied that in respect to the Confederacy the opinions of statesmen, public writers, and military critics were erroneous. We are wise after the event, but what is the use of history if we are not to be instructed by it? Yes; but it may be asked of what use is history if it does not offer more certain instruction than it did in respect to the Confederate war? If others were mistaken why do we especially blame the Confederate Administration? This is our reply. We complain that the Confederate Administration paid no heed to the lessons of history; and we assert that if the condition of affairs had been as well known in Europe as it was to the Confederate

Administration there would have been few believers in the success of the Confederacy, even in the heyday of real or apparent prosperity. It is, then, no excuse for the Confederate Administration that the conclusions of foreigners were wrong. The conclusions of Europeans were false because the suggested premises were false. Nor is this all. It is possible that in 1862 it might have been thought that the Confederacy had a chance of success, even if the true state of affairs had been known; but no one would have done so if the policy of the Confederate Administration had been foreshadowed. Whether the Confederacy could possibly have succeeded may be an open question, but we think it can be shown that with the policy adopted by the Confederate Administration failure was inevitable. We repeat, that it concerns the honour of the South and of the North, the well-fare of the United States, and must interest all peoples to investigate the causes of the fall of the Confederacy, for nothing can be more injurious and more unfounded than the assumption that the catastrophe was immediately and solely due to the superior numbers of the North. We assume that, despite the numerical superiority of the North, the Confederacy had a chance of life, at least of a longer life than four years. How was that chance lost? Why was the Confederacy utterly destroyed in four years? What were the immediate causes of the early and sudden decease?

CHAPTER II.

THE REVOLUTION WAS UNTIMELY.

THE revolution was a surprise. The fathers of the Republic dreaded the growth of sectionalism and the disruption of the Union, but if they could have foreseen the condition of affairs in 1860, no such fear would have marred their joy in the prospective glory and greatness of their beloved country. Many writers had prophesied the break up of the Union, but if we examine these predictions we find they had no better foundation than the dogma that mortal things must change, and that nations, like men, must grow old and decay. On this assumption, over and over again, the decline of England has been announced, but though such prognostications alarm the timid, they do not obtain credence, except with those who maliciously wish the evil to come to pass. Secession had often been threatened both by North and South, but everyone knew that these threats were rhetorical exaggerations, for even whilst they were being bandied about in the halls of Congress, on the platform, and in the press, all parties and sections were zealously, jealously, and it often seemed unscrupulously, striving to aggrandise the Republic. The people of the North and of the South, of the East and of the West, equally regarded America as the heritage of the Union, and looked forward to the day when the lord of the White House would be the chief magistrate of a Continent.

But however uncertain the future, however probable that ultimately North and South would separate, there was no premonitory sign of immediate divorce in 1860. Revolutions are usually the result of long-continued oppression. The more we study the French revolution, or the English revolutions, or the Italian revolutions, or the revolts of the Poles, the more we marvel at the cruel and persistent folly of tyrants, and at the long suffering of peoples. The Southerners were socially and politically as free as they had ever been or ever could hope to be. They were subject to equal laws impartially administered. They had their full share of national honours. Besides, in 1860, they had taken part in a great act of union. They had participated in the election of a President. Was it likely that a people who to-day accepted an appeal to the ballot-box would to-morrow, if defeated, appeal to revolution!

The secession was a surprise not only to Europe but to the South. If it had been contemplated the people would have scorned to assist in the Presidential election. They would have acted honourably and more wisely. They would have said to the North, "we shall not vote in this Presidential election because it may be that we should be unable to abide by the result. We regard Abraham Lincoln as the representative of a sectionalism antagonistic to the South. If you elect him we shall secede." To affirm that the revolution was not a surprise to the South is to brand a whole people with an infamous violation of a most solemn contract. To suppose that the

South took part in the election of 1860 with a preconceived idea of repudiating the result in the event of the Southern candidate being defeated, is to charge the people with being guilty of shameful and criminal treachery. We indignantly reject the suggestion. We declare that the countrymen of Lee, and Jackson, and Stewart were incapable of such conduct. Yes; the revolution was a surprise to the South. On the day that Abraham Lincoln was elected there were not five hundred men who dreamt of secession, and probably not fifty who designed it.

A conspiracy was the germ of the revolution. This is not in itself a reproach, for all revolutions begin with conspiracy. But there was a peculiarity about the Southern conspiracy. It did not consist of the leading men, but of the politicians who are called wire-pullers in America. These men were without public repute, but as electioneering agents their power was considerable, so that they were able to coerce the leaders and to lead the people. For example, Mr. Stephens, who afterwards became Vice-President of the Confederacy, vehemently opposed secession, and Generals Lee and Jackson reluctantly submitted to it. But it is not our purpose to pursue this topic. Undoubtedly the revolution was a surprise, but it does not therefore follow that it was premature. That, however, is an important point. Was the revolution well timed or untimely? Granting that Mr. Lincoln was a Sectional President, and that his election was a danger to the South so imminent as to necessitate a dissolution of the Union, was immediate secession expedient? We reply that it was inexpedient. We contend that the revolution was untimely, and that its chances of success were materially impaired by precipitate action.

The South was not prepared for revolution. We do not refer to preparations for war, for in this respect it may be argued that the North was also unprepared. It was of greater consequence that the people were not morally ready for revolution. They had suffered no practical wrong. The consequence is, that the revolution lacked the peculiar power of endurance that is incident to revolutions. The Southern people did their best for the Confederacy, but more would have been done if the revolution had been instigated by the sting of actual grievance. There is a vast difference between fighting for a government and fighting to vindicate right and to defend assailed liberty. Hence, too, the revolution that was invoked to support the Confederacy died before the Confederacy. If there had been an actual wrong to resent, the revolution would have survived the surrender of the Confederate army, and the last ditch would indeed have been contested.

Great would have been the gain of waiting. Was the election of Mr. Lincoln to prove harmless? Then there was no need for secession. Was Mr. Lincoln to strike at the rights of the South? Then the first blow would have nerved every Southern arm to defend the threatened right.

This precipitancy had a disastrous effect on the conduct of affairs. It led to the revolution being treated as a Constitutional movement. A revolution was formally declared, and formally accomplished, but it pleased the Confederate Administration not only to misrepresent the character of the movement, but they showed by all their acts that they believed the fiction that they published. It was solemly averred, that the formation of a Southern Confederacy was not an act of revolution. The Southern States had just engaged in the election of a Chief Magistrate for the United States, and did not dispute the legal and constitutional validity of the return of Mr. Lincoln. They set up a new and distinct Government, and they raised armies to defend the new Confederation; yet we were told that this Confederation, eighty days old, which had seceded from a Federation more than eighty years old, was not a revolutionary Government. The Confederate leaders shrunk from the word revolution as from a hell-blast, at the time they were attempting the greatest revolution of the century. They asserted that the Constitution of the United States did not forbid secession. Perhaps not. They assserted that the Federal Government could not oppose secession without violating the Constitution. Let that be granted. Suppose, for arguments' sake, we admit that the Southern secession was constitutional, and that the opposition of the North was unconstitutional, still it was a revolution for the South to leave the North, and to set up a new and independent Government. Admitting for a moment that secession did not violate, but was sanctioned by the letter of the Constitution, it does not render secession less revolutionary, though it renders the revolution constitutional. The great revolutions that the English race have been engaged in, were Constitutional revolutions. We suppose the movement that made Oliver Cromwell Protector of England, *vice* Charles I. beheaded, was a revolution; yet it must be confessed that, during the first years of the struggle at all events, the revolutionary Roundheads were defending, and the Royal Cavaliers were violating, the tenets of the Constitution. The movement that drove James II.

into exile was a revolution; yet the revolutionists were very particular in adhering to the Constitution. So, when the Thirteen Colonies revolted, the movement was at first in strict accordance with the letter, and, we may add, with the spirit, of the Constitution. Herein is the radical difference between a Constitutional and a Despotic government. Under the latter, a people have no political rights, and therefore resistance to tyranny, no matter how needful, is unconstitutional. Now, Constitutional government is in theory based on the consent of the governed; and, therefore, so much power is vested in the people, that a revolution, whether justified or not, may be constitutional, or, at least, it may not violate the letter of the Constitution. For all practical purposes, the Constitution of England as broadly, perhaps more broadly, involves the right of revolution as does the Constitution of the United States. Free government is a compact in England as in America, and the right to dissolve the union or compact is as valid in England as in America. Suppose the House of Commons refused to pass the Mutiny Bill, to vote the military and naval forces, and to grant the required supplies. Suppose a new Parliament called, and that the new House of Commons followed the example of its predecessor. Suppose it refused to grant supplies until the Sovereign had abolished ecclesiastical titles, or abolished the House of Lords, or declared the Crown elective. The conduct of the House of Commons would be in accordance with the letter and the forms of the Constitution. The letter of the Constitution does not in any way limit the money-power of the House of Commons. Yet such conduct would be revolutionary. What could the Sovereign do? Oppose it? We could not blame the Sovereign for doing so, yet the Constitution does not confer any power upon the Sovereign to oppose such an arbitrary proceeding on the part of the Commons. Every step in defence of the rights of the Sovereign, would necessitate a breach of the Constitution. But this position is not peculiar to England It is in the very nature of a free government, that revolution is not forbidden by the letter of the Constitution. In all governments both free and despotic, power is derived from the consent of the people, only, in the one case, this power is admitted in theory, and in the other case, the theory is, that the government governs by right divine. Therefore, the right of revolution is implied in all constitutions; and it follows, that, in a free country, whether a revolution be justifiable or not, it can seldom, if ever, be opposed without the infraction of the letter of the Constitution. It was, then, a palpable error to assert, that to break up the Union, and to set up a rival government, was not a revolution. The right of revolution is a Constitutional right, to the exercise of which the English race owes its liberty, prosperity, and glory. There were, perhaps, many reasons why the Confederate Administration put forward such an untenable theory. It was done, perhaps, with the hope of conciliating parties, both North and South, and above all, with the hope of at once obtaining the recognition of Europe. It did not occur to the Confederate Administration, that no one would think of acting upon such a pretext. But, strange to say, the Confederate Government did act upon the extraordinary theory that a revolution was not a revolution, but a strictly anti-revolutionary as well as a constitutional proceeding.

The consequences were disastrous to the Confederacy. The passionate energy, so indipensable to the success of a revolution, was checked and fettered. A new-born nation, struggling for continued existence, was girt about, and tied up with red tape. Never in Europe has officialism been so dominant as it was in the Confederacy. The public offices in Richmond would have charmed a Civil Service martinet. We, in England, do not despise red tape, which may be useful enough in time of peace, but we break through the official net in the hour of trial. But the Confederate Government—a Government yet in embryo—adopted and observed all the forms of a settled Government in time of profound peace. When we think of this folly, we are reminded of the Pretender playing at being King in Edinburgh, while the armies of the actual King were marching to crush the rebellion. When the Confederacy needed every man for the army, or for the production of food, there was a mighty host of civil service officials. In the midst of war, invasion, and revolution, if any one was called upon to perform a pressing duty, he had to visit bureau after bureau, and to go through more formalities than are dreamt of even in bureaucratic Vienna. The energy that was strong enough to throw down a fortress, was in this manner filtered through miles of official piping, until at length it issued forth in a tiny streamlet, having scarcely force enough to disturb a house of cards. All this was to prove to the world that a revolution was not a revolution, and that to break from an old government, and to set up a new and rival government, was, indeed, an anti-revolutionary proceeding.

In the midst of war and invasion, all the formalities

of the Constitution were to be observed. What difference did it make to the people of the South whether they were conscripted and pauperised according to the forms or in violation of the forms of the Constitution? To what a condition was the South reduced. The most despotic government could not have inflicted more suffering; but the willing sacrifices of the people, intended for the altar of national Independence, were offered at the shrine of the lying idol Ceremony. Cromwell and his adherents did not suffer their cause to be lost for forms' sake. They were slow to enter upon revolution, they were slow to begin war, but after the struggle commenced, they did not waste their energies in the observance of constitutional ceremonies. There was a time for protesting and then they would not fight, but when the Rubicon was crossed and the fight began they would not stop to parley. They would not permit any constitutional formality, however good in its way, to hinder the momentous work. Did the mace obstruct the march? Then away with the bauble! Did the House of Commons, which began the work, threaten to prevent its completion? Away, then, with the House of Commons! How different it was with the Confederacy. The vessel was in the midst of an awful storm, but not a spar must be cast overboard to lighten her. The vessel was fast drifting on the rocks, but not a sail must be furled. Breakers were ahead, but the sailors must not move hand or foot to save the ship until they had been piped on deck, and until their jackets and sou'-westers had been duly inspected, according to the regulations. It was necessary to be excessively particular. The slightest infraction of official or constitutional etiquette might have raised a suspicion that to separate from an old Federation, and to set up a new Confederacy, was a somewhat revolutionary proceeding.

Braver officers never drew sword than those who led the Confederate armies; yet some Confederate generals were of inferior capacity, or, which is the same in effect, they were unfortunate. Yet they were permitted to retain important commands. Ability had to give place to seniority. There was an outcry, but official etiquette was deaf to it. The people were disgusted, and the army was decimated by desertion. But secession was not a revolution, and anything was better than a disregard of the latest edition of the United States' army and navy lists, and that the ranking officer should be superseded by the best man.

In the South, as in every other country, there was much human carrion. Never was corruption more rife or more impudent. The army of contractors and persons of that class plundered the people shamefully and openly. Angry remonstrances from every State and from every county were unheeded. The Executive hated corruption, but how could it interfere? The Government could not proceed except according to the forms of the Constitution, and in the midst of revolution, war, and invasion, the Constitution was practically in abeyance. The Supreme Court was not even constituted. *Inter arma silent leges.* So the contractors robbed the people with impunity. Now, the Confederate Administration would not have thus acted if the revolution had not been so hurried as to make it necessary, for the quieting of conscience, to treat a revolution as a Constitutional movement.

Another ill result of this precipitancy was that it discredited the motive of the Southern people. It was alleged that the revolution was necessary for the defence of the monetary interests of the South. It was alleged that the manufacturers of the East intended, by a protective tariff, to impose upon the agricultural South. But was not the West agricultural as well as the South? Are not the manufacturers a minority, even in the East? If, then, it was a question of free trade, it was by agitation and not by revolution that the South should have proceeded. In respect to fiscal policy, the interests of the South and of the West were so identical that it was expected the West would side with the South. But every one knows that it was not a fiscal question that had brought about secession. It was the negro slavery question. The original promoters of secession did not apprehend any attack upon the institution as it existed in the then Slave States, but they feared that the area of negro slavery would be limited to the then Slave States, and they determined to resist a policy they deemed fatal to an institution which they regarded as essential to the prosperity of the country. Now, the mass of the people in the South were personally indifferent to the institution. The slaveholders constituted a small minority, and the majority had no more direct interest in the institution of negro slavery than the bulk of the people of England have in the law of primogeniture. Not that the people of the South were prone to abolitionism. They had always lived in the midst of negro slavery, and had no thought of its being an evil institution. Therefore, in one sense, they fought for the defence of negro slavery, but they did so because they were persuaded that any attack upon the institution was an attack upon the rights of the South. They fought for negro slavery because they were instructed that the defence thereof was indispensable to the defence of their political independence. Hence, when Mr. Lincoln offered to receive back into the Union, with the institution of negro slavery intact, any State that would lay down arms by the 1st of January, 1863, not one of the States accepted the offer. Why? Because they were bent on independence and not on the defence of negro slavery; just as the North, which accomplished the work of emancipation, was intent upon the preservation of the Union, and would, at any time in 1863, have received back the South with the institution of negro slavery as it was in 1861. But, because no other motive could be conceived for the precipitate revolution, it was naturally assumed that the sole object of the Confederacy was to set up a slave empire. This united West and East against the South, and impaired the Confederacy in the eyes of Europe. If the revolution had been delayed until the South had received some practical injury from the North, there would not have been such a serious misconception as to the motive of the people.

Yes, secession was a surprise to the South and to all the world. It was so premature that the revolutionary energy of the people was undeveloped. It was so uncalled for by any act of the North that, in self-defence, the Confederate Administration had to assert that a revolution was not a revolution, and to treat it as a constitutional movement. It was so hurried that it appeared as a conspiracy to set up a slave empire, even after the conspiracy had become a revolution. The revolution was a surprise, and it was untimely; and this is one reason why it did not succeed, and why the Confederacy, which it was invoked to support, did not endure.

CHAPTER III.

THE WAR WAS PRECIPITATE.

SECESSION being formally effected, was immediate war inevitable? We do not ask whether the South had a fair excuse for war. We do not ask whether the attempt to reinforce Fort Sumter was or was not a legitimate *casus belli*, for even if the North was guilty of an act of hostility, it does not follow that the South was bound to retaliate. When a nation is inclined for war, there is never a difficulty in finding a pretext; nor when a nation wants to maintain peace is there often an insuperable difficulty in satisfying the national honour without an appeal to the sword. It was, we presume, the special business of the Confederate Government to protect and foster the new-born Confederacy. We think it will not be denied that the Confederate Government embraced the first possible pretext for war. We do not discuss the morality or the immorality of so doing. We have to consider whether it was politic thus to plunge into hostilities.

Before the fall of Fort Sumter the North was by no means united in opposition to secession. A large and daily growing party was in favour of letting the South go. Not that this party dreamt of an actual and final dissolution of the Union. It was known that in every Southern State, perhaps, with one exception, there was a powerful Union party, and it was supposed that a separation would be temporary; and that in a few years, probably in less than a Presidential term, North and South would be again under one general government. Nor was this supposition unreasonable. Notwithstanding the excitement incident to revolution, the wire-pullers and managers of the secession movement had to resort to innumerable manœuvres to secure majorities. Flying election cavalry was employed, so that the same votes were recorded at half-a-dozen booths in succession. The most positive assurances were given to the pro-unionists that secession was only a protest to save the Union. Pro-secessionists were assured, with equal positiveness, that England and France were pledged to an offensive and defensive alliance. Still, there were formidable minorities voting against secession; and in every State there were numbers who would not vote. The smallest concession on the part of the North would have converted the neutrals into active opponents of secession; and it is not doubtful that in most of the States their adhesion would have changed the pro-union minority into an immense majority. Added to this the Secession camp was crowded with waverers. Many who voted for secession did it as a kind of protest, and with no idea of setting up a rival power to the cherished Union. It was, therefore, we say, not unreasonable for the North to suppose that a separation would be temporary.

Even the temporary separation was not to be a virtual dismemberment of the Union. There were to be two Presidents and two Congresses, but an identical commercial and foreign policy. For a few years, in lieu of a union of States, there was to be a union of Federations. Likely enough, if secession had been accomplished on any terms, the disunion would have been lasting. But the Northern party, in favour of letting the South go, did not think so, and that party was, before the fall of Fort Sumter, strong and daily increasing in strength.

Mr. Lincoln appreciated the position. When he took the oaths of office there was not a war party, or if so, it was too small to avow itself. Therefore the extreme caution that marked his inaugural address. The Southern States had seceded, but he did not intimate any intention of using force to bring them back into the Union. If secession was illegal, it was treasonable. Well, the treason was undisguised, but Mr. Lincoln said not a word about punishing traitors. He declared that he had no right and "no inclination" to interfere with the institution of slavery in the States wherein it existed. Beyond holding the places and property belonging to the Federal Government, there was to be no assertion of Federal rights in the South. If the custom-houses were not allowed on shore, the dues were to be collected by vessels stationed at the entrances of the ports. If the hostility against the Union was so violent as to prevent resident citizens holding Federal offices, there was to be no attempt to force obnoxious strangers upon the people, and for a time the offices were to be discontinued. If the South desired it, even the postal service was to be suspended. This was denounced as a feeble, and unwise policy. It seemed to be framed to give comfort and assurance to secession. The Republicans, flushed with victory, were annoyed at the deference paid to their defeated political opponents; the Abolitionists were naturally incensed at the emphatic recognition of the pro-slavery rights of the South ; the staunch Unionists were alarmed at the mild treatment of secession, and the Democrats were not pleased with a policy which proposed peace on the basis of a Republican platform. Yet what could Mr. Lincoln do? When he took the oaths of office secession was formally accomplished. Confederate commissioners were in Washington. Still the public mind was not excited, and there was no talk of punishing the "traitors." Nay, the epithet of "traitors" was not then applied to secessionists. This apparent apathy did not arise from any indifference to the fate of the Union, but because the majority thought that secession was a mere pretext, and those who believed in it deemed it temporary, and by no means involving the existence of a rival power. Mr. Lincoln was obliged to be cautious. Any threat might have been ruinous. He therefore adopted the only wise policy, that of masterly inactivity. It was indeed a dangerous policy, but it was successful, because of the impatience of the Confederate Government.

If the South had maintained a pacific attitude, Mr. Lincoln would have been compelled to adhere to his inaugural programme. Any aggression on the South would have stimulated the Southern people, and would have strengthened the pro-secession party in the North. If Mr. Lincoln had made a show of coercion, Tennessee and Kentucky would have been wholly with the South. A few months of delay would have made war nearly impossible. Commercial intercourse between the sections would have continued, and there would have been more and more disposition to let the South secede on certain conditions—the principal one being an identical foreign policy, and a common foreign representation for the two Federations. Every day the extreme Abolitionists were getting louder in their advocacy of secession. It is easy to censure the fanaticism of the Abolitonists, but it is impossible to deny their zeal and oneness of purpose. In March 1861 the dread was upon them that the crisis would pass away, and that slavery would wax stronger than ever in the Union. The Abolitionists yearned for the emancipation of the negroes, and they expected that emancipation would be the result of secession. The separation of the South from the North would be the death-blow of the Fugitive-slave Law, and rightly or wrongly, that law was regarded as the bulwark of the Southern institution. In March 1861 emancipation was more a desire than an expectation. On one point, however, the Abolitionists were determined. Come what would, negro slavery should no longer exist in the Union. The Abolitionists were staunch Unionists, but they deemed it far better to let the South go than that the Union should continue to protect and uphold an institution which they believed to be infamous and accursed. The Abolitionists shrunk from an immediate re-union, for that would have involved the continuance of slavery in the Union. Therefore, especially after the delivery of Mr. Lincoln's Inaugural, the fervent Abolitionists were inclined to support secession as a much less evil than the perpetuation of slavery in the Union, which then appeared to be the alternative. The Abolitionists ardently loved the Union, yet often, in their long struggle against slavery, they had threatened to break up the Federation. It is not encroaching on the domain of speculation to assert that if the Confederate Government had maintained a pacific attitude for a few weeks longer, the chance of the South coming back with the institution of slavery intact would have made the Abolitionists zealous supporters of secession; and be it remembered the abolition element was the life and soul of the Republican party. We do not deny that in March 1861 the terms of separation that were thought of by the Abolitionists and the peace-men, were such as would have been distasteful to the Confederate leaders. The theory was that the separation was to be exclusively domestic, and that before the world North and South were still to be one. Two Presidents, two Congresses, but one tariff, one army, one navy, one flag, and one foreign department. During the war a letter was published, written by a distinguished Abolitionist, condemning the conduct of England in recognising the Confederacy as a belligerent power, and asserting that even if the South prevailed and the North formally acknowledged the independence of the Confederacy, England ought not to do so. This seemed very absurd to those who were ignorant of the peculiar views that had been, and were, entertained about secession; but in the moment of the deepest gloom, and when many were in favour of letting the South depart, it was still thought that the separation would be merely domestic. The Confederate Administration were aware of this sentiment, but with blind impetuosity they denounced it, and in words of pride and bitterness, they scornfully rejected the suggestion of a separation that did not involve the setting up of a rival power to the United States. Who cannot see that a separation on any terms might probably, if the South had desired it, have been, after a few years, changed into an unconditional separation? But we say that if, despite the impolitic rejection of the idea of conditional separation, the Confederate Government had maintained a pacific attitude, the Abolitionists would have been clamorous for an unconditional separation, rather than the South should re-enter the Union with the institution of negro slavery intact.

There was another fear that was upon all parties in the North, in March 1861. It was an article of popular faith in the States that Europe—and Europe meant England—and most likely France and Spain, would be delighted at the breaking up of the Union, and that if the South seceded the European Powers would joyfully accept an offensive and defensive alliance. That was dreaded as a mortal blow to the supremacy of the revered Union. Therefore, in March, 1861, there was a universal agreement that nothing should be done to incense the South and to induce her to listen to the overtures of Europe. The cry of "no coercion" was heard on every side. Now, if the Confederate Government had waited for a few weeks the suspense would have rendered this apprehension about European intervention more and more intense, and any and every show of aggression on the part of Mr. Lincoln would have been denounced as a fatal blunder by which the South might be thrown into the arms of England and France, and the integrity of the Union put in great jeopardy. Why, if the South had remained pacific for a few weeks, and if, when Fort Sumter was reinforced, or some other aggresssion had been effected or attempted, the Confederate Government had protested energetically, and had besought the North not to force the South to look to foreign alliances for the defence of her rights, the protest would have been almost fatal to the Lincoln Government.

Very critical was the position of Mr. Lincoln, and apparently very forlorn the hope of saving the Union, in March, 1861. Secession was formally accomplished. Confederate commissioners were in Washington and were being received with cordiality by leading Northerners. An idea, probably delusive, and certainly embarassing, was prevalent, that a separation would not be final, that it would be merely domestic, and that there would be, *pro tem*, in lieu, of a Union of States a Union of Federations. If the Union was not to be broken up slavery must be maintained, and the Abolitionists were, in tones of thunder, declaring that their should be no more slavery within the borders of the Union, and that it was far better for the South to depart in peace. All parties were anxious about Europe, and for fear of the intervention of England and France, there was a disposition to let the South secede in amity. If secession was treason, Mr. Lincoln was forced to wink at it. The envoys of the Confederate Government were in Washington, and yet Mr. Lincoln could not arrest them. Newspapers were defending secession but they were not prosecuted. Mr. Lincoln did not intimate, in his memorable Inaugural, that the leaders of secession, and the members of the Confederate Government were to be punished for their proceedings. Nay, Mr. Lincoln did not intimate that secession was to be put down. All he intended to do was to collect the customs at the ports of entry, and to hold the Federal property in the Southern States. He would not enforce Federal officers on the South, he would not even enforce the

Federal postal system. It was certainly a weak policy; but what could Mr. Lincoln do? The effect of a strong policy would have caused such dissension in the North that the Union would have been ruined. Could this drivelling policy save the Union? Certainly not, but it was the best policy for the moment.

The situation was unprecedented. A revolutionary movement was formally accomplished. The agents of the revolutionary government were in the Federal capital. They were not only tolerated, but received with honour. Mr. Lincoln dared not threaten to punish secession, but, on the contrary, he treated it with the utmost gentleness. He would only perform on the South the offices expressly enjoined in the Constitution, and would allow some of these to be in abeyance, rather than provoke a conflict. The Abolitionists were advocating secession rather than the retention of the South with the constitution of negro slavery intact. The mercantile community was averse to war. The anti-war party in the North was an overwhelming majority. The Confederate Administration had nothing to do but wait. Every day the pro-secession party in the North grew stronger. A little more delay and suspense and the fate of the Union might have been sealed. But those who desired its dismemberment rescued it from the imminent peril. At the critical moment the South drew the sword, and the Union was saved—saved at least from the danger of dissolution without a struggle. The booming of the Confederate cannon against Fort Sumter, was the knell of the Confederacy. We do not mean to assert that the contest was hopeless. The revolution was untimely; yet as we have just seen, it had a chance of success, and might have succeeded if the war had not been precipitate. So, too, although the war was precipitate, there might have been a prospect of ultimate triumph. But it is indisputable that by rashly beginning or accepting war, the Confederate Administration gave up a strong and winning position, and staked everything upon the necessarily doubtful issue of an appeal to force.

The South fired the first gun in anger, and all was changed. Nor can we be surprised at the effect of this proceeding on the North. When Fort Sumter fell, Mr. Lincoln ceased to be the representative of a party, and became the chief of a nation. The voice of Faction was hushed, and the spirit of Party was quelled. The Abolitionists, who had been disposed to lose the South, rather than retain the South with negro slavery, saw an opportunity of preserving the Union they loved, whilst destroying the institution they hated. Those who had been apathetic in respect to secession, because they regarded it as a temporary, and only a domestic separation, became, on the instant, staunch and uncompromising opponents of secession, when they saw that secession meant the setting-up of a rival power. Those who had been opposed to coercion, lest the South should be forced into an alliance with Europe, suddenly perceived that the only sure way to prevent the intervention of Europe, was to keep the South in the Union. The business-men were aghast at the prospect of a rival power that would institute rival tariffs, which might for many years deprive the North of the rich commerce of the South. So long as the Confederate Administration maintained a pacific attitude, it was, or seemed to be, the interest of all parties at the North not to oppose secession by force. As soon as the South fired a gun, it was, or seemed to be, the interest of all parties at the North to fight for the union of North and South. When the rash act of the Confederate Administration opened the eyes of the Northern people, their excitement was intensified by perceiving how nearly they had escaped consenting to the establishment of a rival power, and to the utter blighting of the fond hope of Continental dominion.

How can we explain such a monstrous and fatal blunder on the part of the Confederate Administration? An enemy and detractor might suggest that they rushed into war because it was the only way to hinder the Unionists in the South returning to the Union, and that unless separated by a river of human blood, North and South could not be kept asunder. We reject such an explanation. It would be scandalous to impute such an atrocious motive to the Confederate Administration. We cannot solve the problem. We cannot imagine a plausible excuse for such manifest and disastrous folly.

We can hardly conceive that men who had passed their lives in the political arena of the United States, were beguiled by the moderation of Mr. Lincoln's Inaugural, and by the pacific disposition of the North, and therefore concluded that such a people as the Northerners were to be terrified and subdued by a display of force. And if the Southern leaders had consulted historical precedents, they would have learnt that only those revolutions have succeeded which resorted to war in the last extremity. When, on two occasions, the people of England triumphed over their Stuart kings, their patience was most conspicuous. It was particularly so in the great rebellion which resulted in the death of Charles I. Again and again was the word of the faithless monarch accepted. Flagrant violations of popular rights were submitted to, under firm but respectful protest. Many wrongs were endured before the Commons resorted to arms; and, finally, they did so for defence, and not for aggression. We may be sure that ardent patriots denounced the repeated protests as cowardly, and clamoured for immediate action. We may be sure that when Charles dismissed his Parliament, and essayed to reign without one, it was thought that the hour had come for revolt. But the fathers of the English revolution were wise. They waited until the people felt the practical ills of tyranny. They foiled the king by this waiting. If Charles imagined that their patience was due to pusillanimity he was soon undeceived. He might have won if the Commons had been in haste to wage war; but, unfortunately for him, the patriots were men who had faith to wait for, as well as zeal to use, opportunities. The American colonists followed the example of their revolutionary forefathers. They began with protests, not with revolution. It was only after years of remonstrance and petition, after years of agitation and association, it was only after George III. had struck the first blow, that they issued the famous Declaration of Independence, and prepared for war. This patient waiting for the opportune moment is a mighty power. To be long suffering, to bear with affliction until the cup runs over, and until Providence opens a door of refuge, is the sure presage of ultimate triumph. If, at the outset of the quarrel, the colonists had rushed into war, George III. might have maintained his empire intact. And Europe affords a later and striking illustration of this principle. Charles Albert precipitated a conflict in Italy and he was beaten. Cavour knew how to wait, and the kingdom of Italy is the fruit of his patience.

It may, perhaps, be suggested that the war was inevitable, and that the South merely struck the first blow. And here we may remark, that during the contest, no point was disputed with more warmth, than the question of which side began the war. Why? When the conflict commenced, could it hurt the North to confess that it began the war? Both President Lincoln and President Buchanan—the latter especially—were censured for want of decision. It was said that the Southern rebellion might have been nipped in the bud, and was allowed to attain to maturity. Yet the Northern Administration as zealously affirmed, as the Confederate Administration positively denied, that the South began the war. It did so because even after the war commenced the small peace minority of the North would have been materially increased if it could have been shown that the Federal Government began the war. On the other hand, if the South did so, then, in the eyes of all Union men the Confederate Administration was guilty, not only of secession, but of an attempt to set up a rival goverment. If the South began the war, the Southern people could not but charge the Confederate Administration with throwing away the opportunity of a peaceful solution of the difficulty, and also with rushing into a conflict without adequate preparation. And there can be no dispute that the South began the war. We take it that no one will pretend that the attempt to reinforce Fort Sumter was, under the circumstances, an act of hostility demanding reprisals at any cost.

The precipitate war was a military as well as a political blunder. The North was unprepared, but so was the South, and the peculiarity is this, that so long as the *status quo* continued the North could not prepare for war, and the South could do so. The North was watched by a host of Southern friends, and any preparation for war would have raised a storm that would have been destructive of the Federal administration. Now, the South might in a few weeks have made important preparations for war. Cotton might have been shipped to Europe. Stores, not technically war-stores, though necessary for waging war, such as medicines, clothing, and iron for the railroads, might have been imported. Every hour's delay would have found the South in a better position for defence, while the North would have been unable to venture on any preparations for a conflict. But we must not be surprised that the Administration which threw away a rare chance of victory without fighting, disregarded the military advantages of delaying an appeal to arms.

Possibly some may be of opinion that the revolution was not untimely, but surely no candid inquirer can deny that the war was precipitate.

CHAPTER IV.

THE CONFEDERATE POLICY.

SUCCESS, whether an enterprise be good or bad, is the fruit of merit, and failure is the fruit of demerit. Whatever we reap, that we have sown. It is therefore a righteous instinct that prompts us to pay homage to the victor, and to disparage the genius, or the judgment, or the conduct of the defeated. Not to believe that the reward is according to the work is worse than political atheism, for it implies the belief that there is a supreme but capricious or unjust Providence. But even as men know by instinct that there is a God, so they are persuaded, not by argument, but by an inner consciousness, that there is no partiality in the decrees of Providence, and that in every instance the recompense is according to the desert; and for the vindication and support of this faith in the unerring wisdom and justice of the Deity, as well as for the sake of instruction, it behoves us, without fear or hesitation, to consider the causes of failure as well as the causes of success.

It is exceptionally important to do so with respect to the Confederacy. To shirk the inquiry, on the false plea of generosity to the unsuccessful, is to cast a slur upon the people of the South, or else to vindicate the judgment of the Confederate Administration at the expense of their moral character.

It is possible that the Confederate Administration might tell us that they deplored, but could not prevent, the untimely revolution; and they might assert that the war, whether precipitate or not, was forced upon them. But, however that may be, their subsequent responsibility is not to be gainsayed. When the conflict began, when it went on—homes being desolated and men slain—the Confederate Administration would have been guilty of a crime of unprecedented atrocity if they had not felt convinced that their ultimate triumph was, according to human judgment, certain. Surely no one will be so cruelly unjust to the Confederate Administration as to suppose that they saturated a continent with human blood on what they deemed a doubtful issue. On the other hand, no one will dare to assert that the Southern people failed the Administration. What, then, were the causes of failure? What were the bases of the hope of success? Were those bases inherently weak, or were they destroyed by a weak, and it may be a perverse policy?

The contingencies on which the Confederate Administration relied for success were:—

1. The North giving up the struggle.
2. Disunion in the North.
3. Foreign intervention.

If the combatants were to be let alone, and were to go on until the exhaustion of one of them, the triumph of the North—of the power with greater numbers and resources—was indubitable. Was it likely that the North would give in? There is no example in history of a people relinquishing empire until reduced to the last extremity. Spain and England clung passionately to their American colonies. Had it not been for the European complication England would have persisted for a longer time in the almost ruinous struggle. Spain was in a condition of enervation, yet she fought for her American possessions with pertinacity. If England and Spain contended so resolutely for colonies, for distant dependencies, was it likely that the North would be less resolute in fighting for the retention of territory separated from her by rivers, not by an ocean, and that was geographically a part of her country, even as England and Wales constitute one country? The South does not geographically bear the same relation to the North that Ireland does to Great Britain, but the nearer relation that Scotland does to the rest of the island. It was not merely improbable, it was, according to experience, impossible that the North would give in, and consent to the loss of the South until every effort had been made to preserve the integrity of the Empire. Beyond this there were special reasons for Northern determination. The Confederates declared that they would fight to the bitter end, and that, if necessary, the war should be continued for twenty years. The North never credited these assertions. The lookers on in Europe were amused with Secretary Seward's frequent and positive announcements that the war would be over in 60 or 90 days. Yet Mr. Seward in this only expressed the general opinion of the Northern people. At the beginning they did not contemplate a long or costly contention, and throughout the war, it was supposed that each enrolment and each campaign was to be the last. The revolution was so hurried that the North never believed in it, but felt confident they had to deal with a conspiracy only, that kept down the hereditary Unionism of the South.

Further, to give up the South was to resign the dearest hope and to disappoint the strongest passion of the nation. Every citizen of the United States called himself an American. Southern gentlemen were, not less frequently than Northern gentlemen, chosen to represent the Union at foreign courts. Did they evince any dislike to the dream or prospect of continental ascendency? On the contrary, ignoring the fact that there were other American governments represented at the foreign courts to which they were accredited, they, the representatives of the Washington government, adopted the style of "The American Minister." All sections, all parties, all conditions of men accepted and fostered the grand and pleasing idea of continental dominion—the idea which finds expression in the so-called Monroe doctrine. Why, if there had been no other motive—if unlike all other peoples, the people of the United States had been disposed to part with territory without fighting for it until exhausted—this passion for and hope of continental dominion would have prevented them from so doing.

Nevertheless, it is evident that the Confederate Administration thought it a possible eventuality that the North would give in. They did not attempt to husband means and to protract the war—the resources of the country being lavished on a few campaigns. The supplies of material and of men were straitly limited, yet neither were spared. A Fabian policy was eschewed, and battles were fought in which victory must be barren except so far as it produced a moral effect. The motives of this policy were to impress foreign nations with the idea that the Confederacy was a *de facto* Power, and to persuade the North to relinquish a terrible and costly struggle. There was a great deal said about the North being a trading community, and also about the finances of the North breaking down. Did the Confederate Administration suppose that commerce enervates a people? Are not the English a trading people? Yet they have borne their part in warfare, and have not always been free from the greed of territory and the love of dominion, So far from commerce enervating a nation it fosters a spirit of enterprise, and a spirit of enterprise begets that endurance which so often triumphs over great difficulties and apparently crushing disaster.

The theory of Northern insolvency stopping the war was wild, and at best a two-edged sword that mostly threatened the Confederacy. Did the French cease to war when they were a bankrupt nation? Did the colonists return to their allegiance to the Crown of England when their currency was so depreciated as to be practically all but valueless? Sometimes, not often, an impoverished exchequer has prevented a war; but when empire or nationality has been at stake, war has never been stopped by financial embarrassment. But, setting this aside, the Confederate suggestion of Federal financial exhaustion ending the war was exceedingly curious and ill-advised. The financial resources of the North were greater than those of the South, and the Confederate treasury was sure to be depleted before the Northern treasury. If financial difficulty was to decide the issue there was no hope for the Confederacy. In proportion as the Confederate Administration relied on the North giving in, they underrated their opponents; and to underrate the strength of an adversary is a foolish and very frequently a fatal blunder.

Still more unfounded was the hope of Federal disunion. To depend on this was to discount the results of victory. It was to rely on a probable consequence of victory as an aid in the fight. If the Confederacy had triumphed, the further disintegration of the Union was not impossible; and this, by the way, which was so constantly paraded by the Confederate press, could only stimulate the North to renewed exertions to prevent a disunion that would produce further disunion. It is not in the time of war that federations fall to pieces, and this the Confederate Administration should have considered. Why was it that in the Congress and in the press of the United States there was kept alive a constant jealousy of Europe? Why, in the hour of civil dissension, were there mutterings against England? It is no secret that in bygone days the threat of a foreign war was regarded as the remedy for symptoms of disunion at home. If there was a chance of the West joining the South, or of the Border States uniting with the Confederacy, secession should have been delayed, or at least war should have been postponed. When war was begun there was no chance of the West or of the Border States going over to the Confederacy. Having enlisted under the flag of the Union, a junction with the Confederacy involved the scandal of desertion. War, no doubt, put in abeyance Unionism of the South, but it also intensified the Unionism of the North. This was not considered by either side. Mr. Seward did not perceive that the war had changed the "gulf conspiracy," into a revolution and a popular movement. The Confederate Administration did not perceive that, as usual, war for the defence of Empire had, in the North, strengthened the bonds of Union. There was, we repeat, a probability that if the Confederacy triumphed the Union would be split up into two or more federations; but the probable results of victory could not help the Confederacy, and, indeed, were in this case more likely to help the North. Instead of predicting further disunion, it would have been prudent for the Confederate Administration to have concealed a danger that must needs have inspirated the North to fight on whilst there was a dollar in the treasury and a man to be enlisted. It was an excess of candour to perpetually assure the North that the establishment of the Southern Confederacy would bring about the secession of the Western States.

Curiously enough, whilst the Confederate Administration to some extent calculated upon a division in the North, and whilst it was of course their policy to promote disunion, they did many things that were sure to embitter North, East, and West, and all classes against the Confederacy. It was supposed that the merchants and traders of the North were kindly disposed to the Confederacy. What was the conduct of the Confederate Administration? They sent forth cruisers to capture and destroy Northern shipping. Now these exploits had not the slightest influence on the progress of the war. They did not add to the military strength of the South, or detract from the military strength of the North. The only effect they had was to incense the commercial community, and to make the merchants of the North the implacable foes of the Confederacy. Then, how did the Confederate Administration deal with the West? The Western States were exhorted not to injure their best customers. They were told that it was their interest to ally themselves with the free-trade Confederacy, and that they might grow rich by supplying the South with bread-stuffs, whilst the South devoted her labour and skill to the cultivation of exportable produce. Simultaneously, the Western States were selected for raiding expeditions, which alarm and irritate but do not weaken. The West was to desert the North and side with the Confederacy, and yet it was the West that suffered most from hostile incursions. It is not very extraordinary that the West became peculiarly vindictive against the Confederacy.

One more illustration of this perverse policy. The Northern peace party, nearly destroyed by the fall of Fort Sumter, gradually revived during the years 1862 and 1863. It was, perhaps, never so formidable as some thought it to be; yet it was powerful enough to make the war party uneasy. It was spreading in the West as well as in the Atlantic cities. The Knights of the Golden Circle were a dangerous organization. The peace party did not suggest, and we may add, did not contemplate, complete separation of North and South. It stoutly opposed the policy of the Federal Administration, and clamoured for a truce and negotiations. Now, a truce would have been of immense value to the Confederacy. The pause would have given the South an opportunity to recruit its strength—for the Confederate armies were depleted more by want of rest than by death and wounds. The moral and political effect of a truce would have been favourable to the Confederacy both in America and Europe. It would have been, indeed, a *quasi* recognition of the Confederacy as a *de facto* Power, since a truce for negotiation is not usual in rebellion or civil war. Besides, any negotiation must have produced violent differences in the North. The peace party were for peace on any terms short of complete separation. They were ready to uphold all the rights and privileges of the South, and to offer fresh guarantees for the maintenance of the institution of negro slavery. It was so notorious that the New England States would not consent to any such terms, that there was talk of the secession of New England—of leaving New England out in the cold. It was tolerably certain that the peace party would have been too feeble to carry out its programme, and the defeat of its candidate for the Presidency, General McClellan, was almost a foregone conclusion ; yet it was of importance to the Confederacy to help the peace party, and, so as far as possible, to divide the North. But what was the course of the Confederate Administration ? At the critical moment they denounced the peace party—the Northern Democracy—in an abusive strain, rare in the bitterest controversies. The war party laughed at the grotesque position of their political opponents, and the Democratic party was shocked, paralyzed, and suffered an overwhelming defeat. The Democratic party was spurned by the Confederate Administration, and henceforth there was not an anti-war party in the North. Surely such rashness on the part of the Confederate Administration is unexampled, yet the facts are indisputable. We hold that there was no foundation for the hope that the Federation would disintegrate during the war. It was, however, a hope entertained by the Confederate Administration, and it was unquestionably their policy to do what they could to foment division in the North. Yet, as we have seen, they did what they could to irritate North, West, and East, and to unite all classes, and all parties against the Confederacy. They extinguished the feeble hope of Northern disunion by a perverse policy.

The main reliance of the Confederate Administration was on foreign intervention. It was not mere recognition for which the South was anxious, and against which the North so energetically protested. Formal recognition was desired by the one, and opposed by the other, because recognition pending a civil war is the immediate forerunner of intervention. The Confederate Administration did not, and perhaps could not, hide their dependence upon Europe for ultimate triumph. It was for the sake of the impression on Europe that the Confederate lines were not contracted, by which means the war might have been prolonged. Nor did the expectation of foreign aid fade away until the last. A few months before the Confederate collapse there were overtures of peace. Mr. Lincoln and Mr. Seward went southward to manage the negotiations. The terms offered were all that could be hoped for under the circumstances. The North only insisted upon two conditions. The South was to return to the Union, and negro slavery was to be abolished. If these conditions were accepted, the Southern States were to resume their former position, and there was to be a complete amnesty. Unless the South was triumphant, and could dictate terms of peace, the return to the Union was a necessary condition; and after what had happened, negro slavery could not survive the Confederacy. When these overtures were made the position of the Confederacy was desperate. Its armies could not be recruited, and neither the genius of Lee nor the valour of his troops could much longer resist the ceaseless and increasing pressure of the Federal forces. Why, then, were the Northern propositions rejected? Success was beyond the pale of probability, and, therefore, better terms could not be obtained. Must we charge the Confederate Administration with the prodigious crime of rejecting a fair opportunity of ending a hopeless conflict? If so, we must hold the Confederate Administration morally responsible for every life lost in the war from the hour of the James River conference to the surrender of the Confederate army. Such a charge and such a conclusion would, in our opinion, be uncharitable and false. The error of the Confederate Administration was an error of judgment, not a moral crime. They still indulged in the hope of foreign intervention. When the news of the fall of Richmond reached Europe, a special agent of the Confederate Government was in Paris, engaged in a final effort to obtain intervention.

Of the three contingencies on which the Confederate Administration based their hopes of success, that of foreign intervention was apparently the most plausible. England might get cotton from India, and would not incur the risk of a collision even for the sake of her staple industry; but was it likely that she would not embrace the opportunity of dividing a power that perpetually threatened her dominion in America? Was it not also sure that France, which had aided the formation of the Empire in Mexico, would support the Confederacy? If the Confederacy fell, the Mexican Empire must fall too. Was it likely that the French Government would set up an empire that it did not mean to sustain in the only way it could be effectually sustained? It would be tedious to recount the arguments for and against recognition. We have evidence enough that the expectation of intervention was not utterly unfounded. There was a Confederate party in France. There was a Confederate party in England. It needed apparently but a little, a very little addition to the pro-Confederate sympathy to turn the scale. We will not hazard an opinion as to whether it was in the power of the Confederate Administration to have turned the scale of European sentiment actively in favour of the Confederacy; but, beyond dispute, they refused to adopt a policy that would have converted a host of opponents into well-wishers, and they adhered to a policy that gave the North overwhelming moral force in Europe.

In a word, the policy of the Confederate Administration was perverse in every particular. The hopes of success might have been absurdly weak, but whether weak or well-founded, the policy of the Confederate Administration was adapted to frustrate them. The North was to give up the struggle. Lest the North should do so, the utmost pains were taken to show that the South would form a league with Europe against the supremacy of the United States. The North was to give in, and, forsooth, the Confederate Administration did all that it could to anger, incense, and hurt the susceptibility of the North. Then the North was to divide. The West was to join the South. Did the Confederate Administration seek to conciliate the West? Yes, by raiding in the Western States. The merchants of New York were supposed to be friendly to the South, and therefore the Confederate Administration sent forth cruisers to burn their shipping. There was a peace party in the North, and at a critical moment this party was destroyed by the flagrant insults of the Confederate Administration. Perverse is too poor a word to describe the policy of the Confederate Administration.

The revolution was untimely, yet, as we have seen, there was a prospect of success before the commencement of the war. The war was precipitate, yet there might have been a chance of success but for a perverse policy culminating in a third and fatal error. The Confederate Administration did not emancipate the negroes. This, we say, was the crowning blunder, and those who will be at the pains to examine the question will be persuaded that the Confederate Administration lost the last chance of independence in a vain effort to uphold the institution of negro slavery.

CHAPTER V.

NEGRO EMANCIPATION.

WE were told that the North fought for empire, and the South for independence. It was so. We were told by others that the North fought for emancipation and the South for negro slavery. It was so. The majority of the Northern people were intent on the preservation of the Union, and strange and unprecedented would it have been if they had submitted to the loss of empire without a life-and-death struggle. Mr. Lincoln very well expressed the then popular determination, when he said that he would retain negro slavery to save the Union, or abolish it to save the Union. It must not therefore be supposed that either Mr. Lincoln or the majority of the Northern people were pro-slavery. Not at all. They were resolved that the area of slavery should not be extended by its introduction into the territories of the Union, and they were persuaded that being thus hemmed in there would be negro emancipation at no distant date. No doubt, at least at the outset, with the bulk of the Northern people, the single object of the war was empire, or rather the preservation of empire. Hence, when Mr. Lincoln issued his celebrated proclamation, he did not pronounce for abolition, but rather proclaimed a condition on which negro slavery might be continued. If, in January 1863, the South had chosen to return to the Union, the institution of negro slavery would have been maintained. It is no reproach to the Northern people that their object was empire, for their motive was not the hateful lust of territory, but the defence of an existing empire. Would it be a crime for England to fight for Ireland? Yet Ireland is not, geographically or ethnologically, so nearly allied to England as the Southern States are to the Northern States, and Scotland is not more truly a part of the British dominions than the Southern States are a part of the Federation.

The South fought for independence—for the noblest cause for which woman can weep or man can die. The offer of a return to the Union, with the institution of negro slavery intact was rejected. Not that the Southern people were emancipationists. They were not so far in advance of the Confederate Administration. But just as the Northern people would have sacrificed abolitionism to save the Union, so would the Southern people have given up negro slavery for the sake of independence. If the choice had been presented, "Emancipation of the negro, or submission to the North," the answer would have been all but unanimous, "Away with the institution of negro slavery."

The position was peculiar. The North in intent was fighting for the Union, but it derived great moral and material strength, because it was also fighting for negro emancipation. The South fought for independence, and its weakness was, that whilst the people only thought of asserting their political rights, which they were induced to believe were endangered by continued Union with the North, the cause of independence was, by the policy of the Confederate Administration, associated with the defence of negro slavery.

The losses sustained by the Confederacy by the policy of non-emancipation were many, vast, and inevitable. There was the loss of military power. Slaves could not be conscripted, and if negro conscripts were emancipated, the negro race could not be kept in slavery. It was suggested there was no actual military loss, because the negroes cultivated the fields, and all the white men were consequently available for the camp. It is not possible to conceive a poorer excuse for a gigantic blunder. No system has ever been devised by which the whole of the fighting population of a State can be enrolled. Besides boys and old men, and the feeble and decrepit, there will always be a host of exempts ample for the purposes of agriculture. So it was in the South and in the North, and so it has always been in all countries. To exempt an entire section of the community, on the ground that the exemption would set free the rest of the community for military service, is an act of folly for which there was no precedent, until it was committed by the Confederate Administration. In ancient times slaves had to fight. In later ages the serfs had to follow their liege lords to battle. What would have been said if the Federal Government had decreed that no men of a less stature than 5 ft. 6 in., or that no men with black hair, or that no men with names of two syllables should be enlisted? Such a decree would have been greeted with shouts of derision, and the Federal Administration would have been taunted as madmen.

Yet the practical result of the non-emancipation policy of the South was precisely what would have happened in the North, if such a mad decree had emanated from the White House. There were 400,000 negroes in the South capable of bearing arms, and the exemption of negroes from military service deprived the Confederacy of not less than 300,000 soldiers. Now, when we reflect how often Southern victories were barren, because there was no reserve force to reap the harvest, how troops needed in the field were obliged to remain in garrison, and how long the issue seemed doubtful, it is hardly presumptuous to assert that if the Confederacy had been supported by 300,000 negro troops, that even though it would not have been ultimately successful, the conflict would have lasted for twice four years, and every year of war multiplied the chances of foreign intervention. If anything were needed to make the military loss sustained by the South through the policy of non-emancipation more striking, we have it in the fact that the North adopted a policy of emancipation, and that the Northern armies were recruited with Southern negroes. But it is superfluous to recite any other than the one fact, that because the Confederate Administration did not emancipate the negroes, the Confederate armies were deprived of the aid of 300,000 soldiers.

But the physical loss entailed by the non-emancipation policy was small compared with other losses. Was the North to be divided? Was the West to be tempted to forsake the Union? Was the Northern people to give up the costly struggle? Then one obstacle must be removed. The West had no quarrel with the South on fiscal questions, but the West was devoted to the cause of Abolitionism, and would not forsake the North so long as the North included emancipation in its programme, and the South adhered to its non-emancipation policy. It might have been that the North would grow weary of the war; and rather than incur the risk of European intervention, would recognise the Confederacy, hoping that in the days to come there might be reunion. But if so, one obstacle must be removed. So long as emancipation was included in the programme of the North, and so long as the Confederacy adhered to a policy of non-emancipation, the Abolitionists—who before the war preferred to let the South go, rather than have negro slavery in the Union—would have prevented peace on the basis of the dissolution of the Union, because the war for the Union had become a war for negro emancipation. Yes; this question of emancipation, which the Federal and Confederate Administrations and Europe deemed of secondary importance, was all-important. Because the Confederate Administration would not give up negro slavery, it lost the aid of 300,000 soldiers; and because the Federal Administration adopted the policy of emancipation, it kept the West loyal to the East—loyal, we mean, not only as part of the Union, but in the sense of being zealous and unanimous in the prosecution of hostilities against the Confederacy.

We have said that the Confederate Administration relied mainly for success on foreign intervention. We desire to offer no opinion as to whether recognition—which is another name for intervention—would have followed from negro emancipation, or even whether foreign intervention would have secured the triumph of the Confederacy. But no one will deny that negro slavery stood in the way of recognition. And when we remember what an influential pro-Southern party there was both in England and France, and how the friends of the North met every argument put forth on behalf of the South, by reminding us that the Confederacy upheld the institution of negro slavery, there is some sense in supposing that if the South had adopted the policy of emancipation, the hope of foreign intervention might not have proved so utterly fallacious. Yes; at every turn this negro slavery question meets us. The more we reflect the more thoroughly we are convinced that the war for Empire and for Independence was really a war of emancipation. The Confederacy adhered to negro slavery and failed. It might have won if the negroes had been emancipated. The North adopted the policy ot emancipation, and won; and despite her numerical resources, might have been beaten but for the policy of emancipation. We are persuaded that the North would not have been so soon—if ever—triumphant, without conjoining the cause of emancipation to the cause of the Union. Perhaps this may be debateable ground; but it is, we submit, manifest that the Confederacy lost much material, political and moral, force by a policy of non-emancipation, and that whether the Confederacy might or might not have triumphed if the negroes had been emancipated, the non-emancipation policy of the Confederate Administration rendered triumph impossible.

Are we deceived as to the motive of secession? Was independence a pretence? Was the motive of the revolution the defence of negro slavery? Was the desolating war waged to keep the coloured race in fetters? We know it was not so. We know that there was no wavering in respect to independence. We know that the offer of the retention of negro slavery, on condition of a return to the Union, was rejected. We know, too, that in the last extremity the Confederate Administration was ready to give up negro slavery, if by that means the Confederacy could be saved. But when we grant, as we must do, that the South fought for independence, it seems monstrous that the Confederate Administration did not adopt the policy of emancipation. To adhere to the institution of negro slavery was to sacrifice at least a third of their military strength, was to make the West an unswerving foe, was to raise a formidable obstacle to foreign recognition, and was to render immediate foreign intervention impossible. As the war went on, non-emancipation became more and more glaringly impolitic. It was bad enough whilst the Federal Administration hesitated, but it was incalculably worse when the cause of negro emancipation was allied to the cause of the Union; for then the North gained many advantages over their opponents, and strength was added to strength. It might have been supposed that at length the eyes of the Confederate Administration would have been opened, and that the emancipation moves of the North would have been met by counter emancipation moves. When Northern armies were recruited by Southern negroes it is inexpressibly strange that the recruiting for the North was not promptly stopped by enlisting the negroes in the Confederate armies. When it was seen that the sympathy of Europe was chilled because the North proclaimed negro emancipation, and the South upheld negro slavery, it is truly marvellous that the Confederate Administration did not declare that an emancipation policy was indispensable to the success of the Confederacy, and decree the freedom of the negroes.

In all this may we not—must we not—reverently perceive the will of God controlling the purposes of man? The North entered upon the struggle and continued it for the defence of empire, but in time made the war for the Union become also a war for negro emancipation. Yes; and so in all human probability gained the victory; for if Abraham Lincoln had refused to decree emancipation, the North would likely enough have been divided, and certainly there would have been great danger of foreign intervention. The South fought for independence, but would not emancipate the negroes, and therefore lost the chance of success. If the North had not loved the Union, secession would not have been opposed, and negro slavery would still have been existent in America. If the South had not loved independence, there would have been reunion in 1863, if not before, and negro slavery would not yet have been abolished. Because the North would not consent to the disruption of the Union, and because the South would not give up the conflict for independence, the negroes were emancipated. Man proposed, and God disposed.

Can we then explain the policy of the Confederate Administration? Yes. The Confederate Administration fought for independence, because they thought that independence would protect and sustain the institution of negro slavery. The Southern people defended the institution of negro slavery because they were told that it involved the defence of their rights and liberties. But if we assume that the Confederate Administration desired independence above all else, their non-emancipation policy is inexplicable. If it is inexplicable, can it be defended? Was there no plausible excuse for the blindness of the Confederate Administration? We unhesitatingly reply there was not a shadow of excuse.

Anyone who had studied the subject must have concluded that negro slavery could not long endure. Its abolition was decreed nineteen centuries ago. When Christ proclaimed the equal rights of all men before God, and the brotherhood of all the families of the earth, the slavery of man by man was doomed. Hard has been the fight—very hard still is the fight. But there has been continuous, and in these latter days, rapid progress. The peoples of France, of Germany, of Italy, and of England, are free. Even in Russia serfdom has been formally abolished, and our children may live to see in that country a despotism replaced by constitutional government. How much of this is due to the example of America cannot be easily estimated. Without the revolt of the Thirteen Colonies, and the establishment of the United States, there might have been a French revolution, but it would have been a revolution of a different type. Well, it was the French revolution, the result of the American revolution, that gave such an impetus to the vindication of human rights, that the heretofore neglected negro became an object of solicitude. To those who fought the battle of emancipation it seemed long, but historically we are struck with the fact that in a generation so great a work was completed. First came the abolition of the slave trade: then, after an interval, ensued the emancipation of the West India negroes. Was America—where men of the English race had set up the Shrine of Liberty when they had gone forth from home and country rather than live under the yoke of oppression—to be uninfluenced by these events? Was America—whose political constitution was declared in the preamble to be founded on the equal and inalienable rights of man—to be unaffected by the progress of freedom and civilization, that had in other lands freed the sons of Africa from pre-historic and unbroken bondage? In America the task was so tremendous that at the outset only a chosen few thought it accomplishable. Yet the men who raised the banner of emancipation in America have lived to behold the cause triumph. How could the Confederate Administration so ignore the signs of the times? Had they not heard of "Uncle Tom's Cabin," and how the author of that book received an ovation in Europe that an imperial victor might have envied? Did they not notice the development of the Abolition party in the North, and how that party had become the right hand and the soul of the dominant party? No doubt the Confederate Administration knew these things, though they did not appreciate their significance. They did not comprehend that to effectually resist the abolition of negro slavery would be to triumph over Christianity itself; for the religion that makes all men equal before God is the uncompromising foe of the enslavement of man by man. Yet the Confederate Administration did unconsciously pay homage to the spirit of the age. The Confederate constitution prohibited the slave trade. That was a blow at negro slavery. It was a condemnation and a brand analogous in principle to that of the Northern Abolitionists, who insisted that the area of negro slavery should be limited to the then existing boundaries, and should not be extended into the territories of the Union. Verily, it was a dire insult to and assault on the institution. If it was wrong to hold negroes in slavery in the territories, it must have been wrong to keep negroes enslaved in the States. And if it was wrong to enslave negroes, it could not be right to keep negroes enslaved. There were a few persons in the South who believed in the abstract right of negro slavery, and they were incensed with the anti-slave-trade clauses of the Confederate Constitution. It is remarkable that the Confederate Administration were not troubled and awakened by the damning incongruity of prohibiting the negro slave trade whilst they upheld negro slavery. They registered the doom of negro slavery whilst they were ready to stake all that they held dear and precious in its defence.

But was there a practical excuse for this perverse policy? Had the Confederate Administration reason for supposing that emancipation would ruin the country? Was there any ground for the assumption that if the negroes were freed they would become an insupportable burden? No doubt some such an idea was prevalent even amongst men who were favourable to emancipation. Abraham Lincoln himself, on one occasion, suggested to a negro deputation that the best course for the coloured race was to emigrate. Yet it can be shown that there was no foundation for this fear, and the Confederate Administration had the best opportunity for knowing that the idea was entirely fallacious.

The negro question has been discussed in a most unsatisfactory and illogical manner. One party has exalted the negro above the white race, whilst the opposite party has pronounced the negro very inferior to the white race, and but little better than the beasts of the field. The truth lies between the two extremes. The negro is not more nor less than a man. Whether or not the African is the physical and mental equal of the European is not the point. Is he a man? Is he a creature of like passions with white men? Is he influenced by the same motives, and is he amenable to the same laws? If so—if the negro is a man—then he must be treated as a man.

The first article in the indictment against the negro was that he is incorrigibly idle. Is this true? Look at the marble palaces of New York. Look at the factories of Lancashire. Look at the commerce in cotton. Behold, these are the products of negro labour. It is the negro of America who has done most to clothe the world. Therefore he will work it appears. Yes; but we are told only as a slave. Why as a slave, yet not as a free man? No one will assert that the negro requires the stimulus of the lash, for those who defended the institution of negro slavery denied indignantly that the negro was ill-treated. Then, if the negro will work for the profit of an owner, it must follow that he will toil when he is to enjoy the fruits of his toil. Ah, the West Indies? Well, what of the West Indies? It is by no means certain that the West Indies would have been prosperous without emancipation, for their prosperity was on the wane before emancipation. Besides, the negro in the West Indies has acted precisely as any other race would have acted. We will take the unfavourable report of an enemy. The negro is represented as refusing to work after his few wants are satisfied. Well, this is not peculiar to the negro, but is common to all races. Labour, mere brow-sweating, is not in itself a blessing, but rather a curse, and no man labours without a motive, that is, without the desire to satisfy a want or aspiration. The Irish are an industrious people. In America, for example, they are singularly prosperous. How are they at home? How many of them are content with a hovel, a pig, and a patch of potatoes? They emigrate, new wants and new aspirations are engendered, and they become industrious. The negro in the West Indies had to contend against an enervating climate, and no pains were taken to stimulate his industry. He has done as well as Irishmen or Scotchmen would have done under the circumstances.

Is the negro prone to idleness? What better evidence can we have of his humanity? In all communities there are men who will not work except under compulsion. What country is without vagrant laws? It is lawful to compel a man to labour, though it is not lawful to take from him the product of his toil. If, then, there was a class in the United States exceptionally prone to idleness—that is, the negro race—the remedy was easy. It was only necessary to adopt stringent vagrant laws; with this special provision, that they were applicable to white as well as to coloured people. It was certain that the power of the State would be as efficacious as the power of an owner, and there would have been no difficulty in compelling the negro to fulfil his labour contract. Besides, there was evidence in America that the free negro would work on the usual conditions. Few employments were open to free negroes, but in those they excelled. As waiters, barbers, and cooks, they were unsurpassed. In the Southern States they were employed as overseers, and no plantations were more profitable than those managed by coloured men. But it is a sufficient reply to the charge of inherent idleness that the negro did work as a slave. The authority of the slave-owner could not be greater than the authority of the State; and a vagrant law, and laws enforcing the fulfilment of labour contracts, will be found far more potent than the fear of the lash. We admit that the negro is disposed to idleness; that is to say, he will not labour after his wants and aspirations are satisfied, and sometimes he will forsake the path of duty for the path of dalliance. Does that prove him to be other than man? No; for it is evidence of his humanity.

The other charges against the negro were that he is devoid of moral sense, and is a savage when not a slave. The negro was said to be predisposed to theft. Well, there are police and prisons in Europe. When we inquire into the facts we find that thieving did not prevail amongst the coloured so much as it did amongst the white population. Nor was this due to the restraints of slavery, for the criminal returns show that the free coloured population of the States yielded less than the average number of criminals. As to social morality, all observers agree that the negroes were fond and faithful in their domestic relations. When we reflect how crime and vice are fostered by ignorance, that the negroes were kept in a state of ignorance, that the sense of responsibility was deadened by the condition of slavery, there can be no doubt that they are not devoid of moral sense, and are, in this respect, the equals of their white brethren.

But the war was a crucial test, and demonstrated the fitness of the negro for social and political freedom. The white men were in the camp ; the negroes were left at home. The property of their masters, the lives and honour of the women and children, were in their power. It was a period of intense excitement. How did the negroes comport themselves ? They were neither negligent nor faithless. They were guiltless of outrage, either on life or on property. They were not incited by the revolution to commit any offences. They were not guilty of the excesses that have disgraced European revolutions. When in the armies of the North they fought as bravely as white men.' Whilst in the South, and before they were liberated, their conduct was prudent and admirable. If they had been guilty of any excesses the cause of negro emancipation would have been hindered. But they were patient and dutiful until the last. Read the story of the French Revolution, and then read the story of the negro emancipation revolution in America. Does the negro suffer by the comparison ?

Is Christianity a cunningly-devised fable ? To those who are Christians we would address the question, How does God deal with the negro ? Has He prepared a special religion, a special means of grace, for the sons of Africa ? No ; He offers the same salvation, on the same terms, to the black as to the white. Does His plan succeed ? The negroes in America are religious, and no churches are more prosperous than the negro churches. God treats the negro as a man, and that is the treatment that he should receive from his fellow-man. The negro is neither more nor less than a man. If persecuted he perishes. If treated with exceptional tenderness he dwindles and decays. The only solution of the negro problem is to follow the example of God, and to treat the negro as a man.

But all that we have here written about the negro was known five years ago, and was especially well known in the Southern States. Therefore it is inexplicable that the Confederate Administration, if they desired to achieve independence above all else, did not adopt a policy of emancipation until it was too late to save the Confederacy. Inexplicable, that is, if we will not confess that there is a God who orders the affairs of man.

The Confederate Administration would not make peace and return to the Union, therefore the negroes were emancipated. The Confederate Administration would not emancipate the negroes, and therefore the chance of establishing the Confederacy was lost. If the Confederate Administration had given up the struggle for independence the emancipation of the negroes would not yet have been effected ; and if the Confederate Administration had emancipated the negroes the Union might not have been saved.

CHAPTER VI.

THE VERDICT.

THE immediate causes of the Fall of the Confederacy were :—

1. An Untimely Revolution.
2. A Precipitate War.
3. The Non-Emancipation of the Negro.

We may well be amazed that the Confederacy existed as long as it did. Without preparation of any kind, either material or moral, and on the morrow of the participation in a solemn act of Union, without the instigation of any wrong, political, social, or legal, there was secession and revolution. That the North persisted in deeming the revolution a conspiracy, and had an unwavering faith in Southern Unionism, is not surprising. Were they to believe in an effect without a cause? The only surprise is that a revolution so rudely torn from the womb of time survived the hour of its birth. But, contrary to all reasoning, expectation, and experience, it did so.

There was a prospect of a pacific accomplishment of secession. The Democrats, smarting under political defeat, being devoted to the extreme doctrine of State Rights, regarding secession as only temporary, and the temporary disruption as domestic, substituting for a while a Union of Federations in lieu of a Union of States, were in favour of letting the South depart in peace. The Abolitionists dreaded nothing so much as continued Union with negro slavery, and not foreseeing that the defence of the Union would bring about emancipation, were not vehemently opposed to secession. All parties deprecated any act of coercion that might compel the South to seek European intervention, and therefore all dealt tenderly with secession, and those who a few weeks later were called rebels and traitors were openly represented by agents in Washington. The situation was so critical that the cause of the Union seemed hopeless. Then the Confederate Administration bombarded Fort Sumter, and the Union was saved, at least, from dissolution without a struggle.

The final and crowning blunder was the non-emancipation of the negroes. By maintaining the institution of negro slavery the Confederacy lost a third of its military strength, it gave East and West a common and exciting cause of enmity against the Confederacy, and it rendered it impossible for the sympathy of Europe to ripen into intervention. The policy of non-emancipation did more than that, for it gave strength both at home and abroad to the North.

Such were the immediate causes of the fall of the Confederacy. What is the verdict? Not *felo de se*, for however unwise and perverse the policy of the Confederate Administration, their desire was to uphold and not to destroy the Confederacy. Perhaps the facts of the case suggest inevitably this verdict:—"The Confederacy was killed, or its death was hastened, by the perverse policy of the Confederate Administration." We cannot gainsay the justice of that conclusion, yet we prefer the open verdict of "Died from natural causes." We prefer it because, though the Confederacy died early, its death was not, in one sense, premature, for the work that the Confederacy had to do was done.

Was the four years' war in vain? Did so many thousands die in vain? Was the heroism of the North and of the South in vain? God forbid that we should think so. God forbid that we should suppose that He does not make all things to work together for good. It is, we trust, not presumptuous, and it cannot be irreverent, if we try to explain the means by the end. Unless we do so, we are confronted by an inscrutable problem that shakes our reliance on human judgment, and pours contempt upon our faith in a Divine Providence.

The North emancipated the negroes, and was victorious; the Confederacy was unsuccessful, and might have been successful if it had emancipated the negroes. However, the war ended, the one-apparently predestined result was negro emancipation. Mark how the means were adapted to this end.

In 1861 the North was not ready for a policy of emancipation. Two years later Abraham Lincoln had to proclaim it cautiously, and under the guise of military expediency. If, in 1861, the South had protested and agitated, instead of seceding, the Abolition party would have been confronted by a formidable opposition, and a compromise would have been effected which would have postponed negro emancipation for an indefinite period. If the revolution had not been untimely, there could not have been a revolution. In 1861 there was a large majority in the North who would have consented to almost any conditions respecting negro slavery in the South, rather than run the risk of breaking up the Union. Consequently, if the ordinary preparations for revolution by protest, by agitation, and by organization had been made, secession would have been arrested by concession, and the negroes would be yet in bondage. If negro emancipation was to ensue, a revolution was indispensable, and a hurried, untimely revolution was alone possible.

Then came the precipitate and impolitic war. If the Union had been preserved by negotiation, the institution of negro slavery would have been continued and strengthened by renewed guarantees. If the Confederacy had been recognised on any conditions, negro slavery would have been let alone. We may be astonished at the impolicy of the Confederate Administration in beginning a war, but war was manifestly a necessity, if the revolution was to result in negro emancipation. The bombardment of Fort Sumter not only saved the Union from destruction, without a struggle to maintain it, but it also prevented the perpetuation of negro bondage, which must have followed from any pacific settlement. The war commences, and the fate of the negro still appears uncertain. If, according to expectation, the conflict had been over in one or two campaigns, whether the North or the South had been victorious, the negro would not have been emancipated; or, if the North had been successful from the outset, it is doubtful if the negro would have been emancipated, even though the war had been protracted. But the South fought magnificently and victoriously, and forced a policy of emancipation on the North for the sake of the Union. If the North had not been devoted to the Union there would have been peace without emancipation. If the South had not been devoted to the cause of independence, there would have been peace without emancipation. The love of the Union, the love of independence, were for a while the conflicting passions that brought about negro emancipation.

The untimely revolution, the precipitate war, the eventful and varied fortunes of the war, were all necessary to emancipation. Then, when the work was done, when the negro was emancipated, the Confederacy died.

It was indeed possible that the Confederacy might have been established if the Confederate Administration had adopted a policy of emancipation. But it was not so, and therefore the emancipation of the negro did not involve the dissolution of the Union.

But the sacrifices were awful enough. What a loss of treasure, what a river of blood, what burning hate, what grief, what agonies did the four years' conflict cost! Let us be thankful that all the afflictions were not in vain, but that they purchased the redemption of a race from immemorial bondage.

Without the revolution the negro would not have been emancipated, and without emancipation the days of the Union were numbered. Every hour the chasm grew broader and deeper. A few years more of Abolitionism in the North, and of negro slavery in the South, and the disintegration of the Union would have been irremediable. North and South, now one people, did not offer up their sons in vain. Without war was there a prospect of emancipation? Without emancipation could the Union have endured?

The battle is over, and it has not left a legacy of hate. Heroically have the people of the South borne with their defeat, for they have accepted it fully; and from the hour that Robert Lee surrendered, they have been loyal to the Union, as their fathers were, and as they were before '61. Heroically has the North used its victory. Not one life has been taken in revenge for the carnage and the cost of the four years' war. Let us pay ungrudging homage to a clemency that has no precedent in the history of mankind. The warfare that rescued a race from bondage, that saved the Union from dissolution, bequeaths not a debt of vengeance, but inaugurates an era of closer and dearer brotherhood.

The fall of the Confederacy teaches important lessons to all peoples. It admonishes us not to resort to revolution until all other means are exhausted, and of the wisdom and duty of waiting for the opportune moment. It warns us not to be in haste to draw the sword, and to put to the issue of battle that which may possibly be achieved by negotiation. It shows how vain it is to resist the progress of civilization and the development of the principles of Christianity. These are some of the lessons to be learned from the story of the fall of the Confederacy. There are many others, and one especially, that it would be a crime for any Christian people to forget or hereafter neglect. The fall of the Confederacy shows how a deadly conflict may end in a real peace, and how the foes of to-day may be brethren on the morrow. These are the means by which this blessed result has come to pass in America. The people of the South nobly and righteously submitted to defeat, and when they ceased to be the armed enemies of the people of the North became on the instant their fellow-citizens, and loyal to the Union. On the other hand, the people of the

North have not tarnished their glory by a single deed of vengeance. Other nations may follow, but to the people of the United States will for ever belong the honour of setting the example of this all-wise and glorious clemency. It constitutes a bond of Union between North and South that Faction cannot fray, and that Treason cannot sunder.

CHAPTER VII.

THE FUTURE OF THE UNION.

THE physician is exceeding watchful after the crisis of a virulent disease. He knows that often the recovery of health is checked by the intervention of minor and too frequently mortal ailments. When the Confederate war was concluded, the thoughtless rejoiced that all danger and difficulty was past, and that on the future there was not a cloud. Not so the statesmen. They were anxious about the future. They saw the possibility of the war being followed by a disastrous political conflict. How was the government of the United States to be carried on? Was there to be the old union on the old conditions? Was there to be the old union on new conditions? On what terms was the South to come back into the the Union?

This last was a troublesome problem. Simple indeed, but involving practical difficulties. By the law of conquest the North had a right to impose fair and reasonable conditions on the South; and the South were bound to accept conditions that were fair and reasonable. But some who arrogated to themselves the proud title of Southern patriots—the men who had not risked their lives for the Confederacy—demurred to this position. They wanted to reverse the issue of the appeal to the sword by quibbling logic. They contended that the North had denied the right of the Southern States to go out of the Union, and therefore the Southern States were in the Union, and did not require re-admission. The reply of the North was this:—"We denied the right of any States to break up the Union, and we assert our right to prevent another attempt to do so."

Yes, the instant that the Confederacy had fallen, there was a renewed clamour about State Rights. The conditions proposed by the North were not oppressive. The amnesty was to be complete and without exception. Not life or liberty or property was to be forfeited. The North demanded no more than the conditions for which they had successfully fought. They insisted only that the perpetuity of the Union should be admitted, and that the emancipation of the negro should be formally and actually completed. Forthwith it was declared that the South ought not to be coerced. The States of the South, it was said, were sovereign States. The North must sacrifice the fruits of victory to the doctrine of State Rights.

This doctrine is a political curiosity. It assumes that a number of independent States are so united and welded together that they have one army, one navy, one general government, one tariff, and one Supreme Court of Appeal, yet that these States are in reality distinct sovereignties, just as England and France are distinct sovereignties. The doctrine of State Rights cannot be confounded with what we in England call local self-government. Nor is it comparable to the principle of the Germanic Confederation. The Germanic Confederation was a number of States in league for certain specified objects. The members of that Confederation did not merge their sovereign rights in the Confederation. They each had distinct governments, distinct armies, and distinct foreign representations. Indeed, there has never been such an arrangement as the State Rights advocates in America contended for. What they dreamt of was a consolidated Empire, comprised of distinct sovereignties. They wanted the United States to be simultaneously united and separate. Such a theory was, of course, utterly impracticable.

Nor did the State Rights party contemplate putting it into practice except in case of secession. It is true they tried nullification, that is they pretended that one or more States might refuse to obey the Acts of the Federal or general government. This claim was however so preposterous, and was so manifestly incompatible with the conduct of government, that after one trial it was altogether repudiated. When next it was deemed necesssary to put in force the State Rights doctrine, it was admitted that a State was indeed obliged to submit to the authority of the Federal Government, so long as it remained in the Union, but that a State could constitutionally assert independence and leave the Union. Nullification was set aside for secession and the doctrine of State Rights practically reduced itself into a right of a part of an Empire being at liberty to separate from the rest of the Empire, if it disapproved of any act of the general government.

State Rights were not the cause of, but the excuse for secession. But for this doctrine the South would not have gone out of the Union. All those who wavered were told that the State was sovereign, and that allegiance to the State was a more solemn obligation than allegiance to the Union. Indeed, it was averred that allegiance to the Union was dependent upon the will of the sovereign State, which had created, and could abrogate it. These assertions induced men like Lee, Jackson, and other good citizens to consent to secession, or rather to accept the consequences of secession.

The reliance placed on this bubble doctrine was marvellous. Europe was to heed and pay it homage. When the English Government recognised the Confederates as belligerents, the Confederate agents asserted, and the North were inclined to believe that it had been done on account of the doctrine of State Rights. It was not so. The recognition of the Confederates as belligerents was simply a recognition of an existing warfare. Throughout the struggle the Confederate Administration vainly endeavoured to persuade the Governments of Europe that the Confederacy ought to be recognised, and at once admitted as a member of the family of nations, because, according to the State Rights doctrine, any State or States might go out of the Union at pleasure.

Let us once more define this State Rights doctrine. A number of States agree to form a common or Federative Government. Not, be it observed, a mere league of States, each State binding itself to contribute a quota of military force in case of need, but a consolidated Republic, having one army, one foreign representation, and one Supreme Court of appeal. Well, these States having so far merged their existence in the Union, assert that they are still separate and sovereign States, and claim the right of going out of the Union if the acts of the Government or of Congress shall displease them. Admit this right and the Union cannot exist. One State is discontented with an act of Congress. "Repeal that act," says the State, "or we go out of the Union." Or, a State wants for its own benefit, a certain law that Congress will not sanction. "Pass that Bill," says the State, "or we will go out of the Union." What follows? Either Congress must submit to the dictation of one or two States or break up the Union. The doctrine of State Rights only needs to be viewed by the light of recent events to be utterly discredited. It implies a form of government that has never been tried. It supposes the United States to enjoy all the advantages of a consolidated Empire; and yet the several States of which the Empire is composed to retain their sovereignty as though the Union was not more than an offensive and defensive league. A more impracticable and dangerous scheme was never propounded. Seeing how it was the excuse for secession—seeing that it can only be upheld as the excuse for secession—seeing that it can never be put into force except by secession, it is necessary for the perpetuity of the Union that the doctrine should be forcibly and distinctly repudiated. We must not be surprised that Congress insists upon this State Rights doctrine being renounced. Otherwise the restoration of the Union is but temporary. If any act of Congress displease the South, or the West, or the East, or the North, then a fourth or a third of the States may secede on the pretence that they have a sovereign right to do so. It must be declared and accepted that the States have no right to go out of the Union, except, indeed, the inalienable right of rebellion or revolution—a right which applies to the component parts of the United Kingdom as much as it does to the component parts of the United States.

When the Confederacy fell, negro slavery ceased to exist within the borders of the United States, but the negro question was not settled. The work of emancipation had to be perfected. The equal rights of the negro had to be decreed. If the suffrage is universal, there is no pretence for denying a vote to the negro. If there is to be a property, or educational, or residental qualification, the test must be applied to white and coloured alike. Nor was it sufficient to decree the equal, social, and political rights of the negroes. It was necessary to provide machinery for enforcing the decree. Not that the white population of the South are unwilling to do justice to the negro, but there are old prejudices to overcome, and the negro, just emancipated, requires some protection. Not help nor even guidance, but protection in the exercise of his rights. Before a single generation has passed away, the Freedmen's Bureau will be unnecessary; it is now indispensable. It is remarkable that there should be any complaint raised on behalf of the South, about giving the suffrage to the negro. For what party will the negro vote? Is the negro so superior to all other races as to be proof against local influence? We may be sure that the negro will vote with the South, not against the South. Now there would have been some reason for the North refusing the suffrage to the negroes. The North might have pleaded: "At present we cannot trust the negroes with the suffrage. Though now emancipated they are not yet free from the influences of a century of slavery. If we give them votes, they will be virtually votes at the disposal of the landowners and other local magnates. For a generation at least, the negro votes would be a weapon in the hands of our political opponents." But the North insists upon the negroes enjoying equal political rights. The Southerners have boasted, and we believe, not without justification, of their influence with the negroes. Now is the moment to test the truth of this assertion. If they have such influence, will they not be able to direct the voting of the negroes? We may marvel at the North insisting upon the equal political rights of the negroes, but we must needs marvel still more at the South objecting to a condition that will add immensely to the electoral power of the South. But indeed it is not the people of the South who object, but the noisy self-delegated advocates, who presume to speak in the name of the Southern people.

Who will settle these differences? Is there any authority that represents the sentiments, the interests, and the power of the American people?

There has been a change in the American Government, not of recent commencement, but which was immensely accelerated by the war. It is a change which ought to rejoice the hearts of the friends of liberty. It is a change that is the best, and indeed the sole guarantee for the maintenance of constitutional freedom. It is a change which has saved the United States from those evil results that might otherwise have followed from the war. We refer to the increased and increasing power of Congress.

In England the struggle for the supremacy of Parliament was long and arduous. It begun in the era of the Tudors. The decisive victory was won in the time of the Stuarts; though the conflict did not then cease. The first sovereigns of the House of Hanover essayed to control the will of the Commons, but happily they were unsuccessful. The Commons may, or may not sufficiently represent the people, but the Commons now enjoys undisputed legislative supremacy. The Sovereign is not possessed of a tittle of legislative power, the right of veto being practically obsolete.

Precisely the same change has taken place in the government of the United States. The authority of the President has declined. Mr. Johnson has vetoed several bills, but they have been passed over his veto, and the action of Congress has been sustained by the nation. By a true instinct the people will not permit one man to rule, but commit, despite the *lex scripta* of the Constitution, supreme power to Congress. Henceforth Congress will rule, and the President will reign. But for that we might, indeed, be anxious about the future of the United States. Wherever there is individual rule, there is virtually a despotism, whether the ruler be called Emperor or President.

The change that has taken place will involve another change. Congress is striving to control the Executive, just as the Parliament of England controls the Executive. This is the inevitable result, when a popular assembly becomes supreme in legislation. The assembly that makes the law will not rest until it has the power and opportunity of enforcing the due execution of its acts. In England, the Executive—that is, the Cabinet—sits in Parliament, where it is ready to answer questions, and to give information. The Cabinet, though nominally chosen by the Crown, is dependent for its existence on the will of the Commons. Hence it is that the division of offices does not interfere with the unity of rule. The Commons not only legislate, but they enforce the due execution of their will and acts. We may be sure that ere long the precedent of England will be followed in America. In every session Congress is more and more inconvenienced by the want of direct relations with the Executive. The government of the country is dangerously enfeebled. There is but one remedy. The ministers must be members of Congress, and they must hold office during the pleasure of Congress. This reform will be one of the immediate consequences of the supremacy of Congress, and it will be accelerated by the contention with Mr. Johnson. For that contention has taught Congress how its acts may be virtually set aside by an Executive that is independent of Congress.

There is another change growing out of the supremacy of Congress that will attract some attention. The office of President of the United States will for ever be one of the highest distinctions to which a man can aspire. But hereafter the President will not be dictator. The altered *status* of the President will necessitate an alteration in the mode of his election. The people vest supreme power in Congress, and it is therefore absurd that they should be called upon to vote for the President. Why should the country be periodically agitated for the choice of an officer who is, after all, inferior in power to the Congress chosen by the people? It will be no small boon to the United States to be rid of the turmoil and disturbance of Presidential elections. Perhaps the most efficient plan would be for Congress to choose a President annually, or every two years, from the six senior members of the Senate, who have not already served the office of President. After the expiration of the term of office, the President would return to the Senate, and therefore a statesman might be Chief Magistrate without putting an end to his public career. But the mode of electing the President is only a question of detail, and relatively unimportant.

What of the future of the United States? Everything depends upon the firmness of Congress and the determination of the people. If Congress wavers in asserting its supremacy, then there may be confusion and disaster. A man cannot serve two masters, and a nation cannot have two rulers. Either Congress or the President must be supreme. The United States must be governed by Congress or by the President. It cannot be governed by both. If the President governs, then the Government of the United States will be practically a dictatorship. Such is not the will of the American people, and they will support the supremacy of Congress.

We need not doubt the firmness of Congress; and, relying on that, there is no apprehension that the Southern difficulty will be lasting. What does the North wish of the South? Only avowed loyalty to the Union, and the complete emancipation of the negroes. Without these conditions are complied with, the Union would perpetually be in jeopardy, as it was in 1860. There ought to be a distinct renunciation of the so-called sovereign State Rights, for that is a doctrine incompatible with a true Union. Nor will the South lose anything by the surrender of this excuse for secession. If she is oppressed, she will have the same remedy that she had in 1861. The North cannot deprive her of the inalienable right of rebellion or revolution. On the other hand, it would be a folly, and worse than a folly for the

North to sanction a doctrine that in 1861 was used to justify the breaking-up of the Union. Then as to the completment of negro emancipation, there is no valid objection. It is not only indisputably just, but pressingly expedient. There is no righteous way to treat the negro but as a man. Let him enjoy equal rights, and he will be easily governed by equal laws.

The future of the United States is radiantly hopeful. The country has come out of the fiery ordeal of revolution and civil war, with power undiminished, and without loss of liberty. So far from the authority of the chief magistrate becoming despotic, as it was prophesied, it has declined. The lessons of the past will not be forgotten. The dangerous doctrine of State Rights will be buried with the Confederacy, of which it was the professedly vital principle. The negro question, which has divided the Union for generations, will be for ever settled by the declaration and enforcement of the equal social and political rights of the coloured race. The supremacy of Congress will be confirmed, and the Great Council of the nation will govern as well as legislate. The liberties of America henceforth will rest on the broad and only safe and enduring basis of the supreme rule of the assembly chosen by and amenable to the will of the people.

THE END.

www.ingramcontent.com/pod-product-compliance
Lightning Source LLC
Chambersburg PA
CBHW021412090426
42742CB00009B/1112

* 9 7 8 3 3 3 7 3 3 0 9 6 5 *